D0846310

Birds *of the* World

DISCARDED
HEGGAN PUBLIC LIBRARY

Volume 2
Birding–Common Moorhen

mc Marshall Cavendish
Reference
New York

MARGARET E. HEGGAN FREE PUBLIC LIBRARY
of the TOWNSHIP OF WASHINGTON
208 East Holly Avenue
HURFFVILLE, NEW JERSEY 08060

Marshall Cavendish Corporation
99 White Plains Road
Tarrytown, New York 10591

www.marshallcavendish.us

©2009 Marshall Cavendish Corporation

All rights reserved. No part of this book may be reproduced or utilized in any form or by any means, electronic or mechanical, including photocopying, recording, or by any information storage and retrieval system, without prior written permission from the publisher and the copyright holders.

Editorial Adviser:
    Jason A. Mobley, Research Associate,
    Cornell Laboratory of Ornithology

Contributing authors:
    Duncan Brewer
    Jonathan Elphick
    Ben Hoare
    Jason A. Mobley
    Mike Unwin
    John Woodward

Marshall Cavendish
    Editor: Evelyn Ngeow
    Publisher: Paul Bernabeo
    Production Manager: Michael Esposito

Discovery Books
    Managing Editor: Paul Humphrey
    Project Editor: Helen Dwyer
    Design Concept: Ian Winton
    Designer: Barry Dwyer
    Cartographer: Stefan Chabluk
    Picture Researcher: Rachel Tisdale
    Illustrators: Stuart Lafford and Malcolm Ellis

Cover: Ruby-throated hummingbird
Title page: Scarlet macaw

The publishers would like to thank the following for their permission to reproduce photographs:
    cover Creatas, back cover & title page Creatas, 68 Jason van der Valk/istockphoto.com, 69 Marcel Pelletier/istockphoto.com, 70 Tony Hamblin/FLPA, 72 Noah Strycker/istockphoto.com, 73 Noah Strycker/istockphoto.com, 74 Sunset/FLPA, 76 Konrad Wothe/Minden Pictures/FLPA, 77 Patricio Robles Gil/Sierra Madre/Minden Pictures/FLPA, 78 Martin Woike/Foto Natura/FLPA, 79 Stockbyte, 80 Malcolm Schuyl/FLPA, 81 Konrad Wothe/Minden Pictures/FLPA, 83 Brand X Pictures, 84 Brand X Pictures, 85 Stockbyte, 86 Susi Eszterhas/Minden Pictures/FLPA, 87 Bill Baston/FLPA, 88 Jan Baks/Foto Natura/Minden Pictures/FLPA, 89 Fritz Polking/FLPA, 90 William S Clark/FLPA, 91 Sunset/FLPA, 92 Tom Vezo/Minden Pictures/FLPA, 93 Stockbyte, 94 Hans Hut/Foto Natura/FLPA, 95 Malcolm Schuyl/FLPA, 96 Bruce MacQueen/istockphoto.com, 98 Ron Austing/FLPA, 100 Michael & Patricia Fogden/Minden Pictures/FLPA, 102 Konrad Wothe/Minden Pictures/FLPA, 103 David Hosking/FLPA, 104 Tom Lewis/istockphoto.com, 106 S & D & K Maslowski/FLPA, 107 S & D & K Maslowski/FLPA, 108 Robert Hambley/istockphoto.com, 110 Pete Oxford/Minden Pictures/FLPA, 112 Jim Brandenburg/Minden Pictures/FLPA, 113 Tom Vezo/Minden Pictures/FLPA, 114 S & D & K Maslowski/FLPA, 116 Michael Durham/Minden Pictures/FLPA, 118 Creatas, 120 Nancy Nehring/istockphoto.com, 121 Randall Royter/istockphoto.com, 122 Tom Vezo/Minden Pictures/FLPA, 124 Tom Vezo/Minden Pictures/FLPA, 125 Ron Austing/FLPA, 126 Tony Campbell/istockphoto.com, 127 S & D & K Maslowski/FLPA, 128 Janet Forjan-Freedman/istockphoto.com, 130 Creatas, 131 Andre Maritz/istockphoto.com, 132 David Hosking/FLPA, 133 Tui De Roy/Minden Pictures/FLPA, 134 Stockbyte, 135 Stockbyte, 136–137 Tui De Roy/Minden Pictures/FLPA, 138 Neil Bowman/FLPA, 140 Gary Martin/istockphoto.com

Library of Congress Cataloging-in-Publication Data

Birds of the world / editorial adviser, Jason A. Mobley.
    v. cm.
  Contents: v. 1. Albatrosses, petrels, and shearwaters--bills and diet --
v. 2. Birding--common moorhen -- v. 3. Conservation--eastern meadowlark --
v. 4. Eggs and young--game birds -- v. 5. Great blue heron--legs and feet --
v. 6. Loggerhead shrike--owls -- v. 7. Parrots and cockatoos--ring-billed
gull -- v. 8. Rock pigeon--storks, ibises, and spoonbills -- v. 9. Swallows
and martins--tufted titmouse -- v. 10. Turkey vulture--wrens and dippers --
v. 11. Indexes.
  ISBN 978-0-7614-7775-4 (set : alk. paper)
  1. Birds. 2. Birds--Pictorial works. I. Mobley, Jason A. II. Title.
  QL673.B573 2008
  598--dc22
                                2008062300

Printed in Malaysia
13 12 11 10 09 08   6 5 4 3 2 1

Contents

Birding

Birding is the art of identifying, observing, and recording birds in their natural environments. Although it is known as bird-watching in many places, the term *birding* has grown in general usage because it more accurately conveys the many dimensions of the activity beyond strictly visual observation—listening to and recording bird sounds, photography, creating art, and managing and sharing field records with others. Modern-day birders devote varying amounts of time and energy to their pursuit but are all united by a passion and excitement for learning more about birds and the natural world.

Birding is an engaging and inspiring activity enjoyed by millions of people of all ages and from virtually all walks of life the world over, and it is one of the fastest growing outdoor activities in North America. In 2006, the U.S. Fish and Wildlife Service reported more than 47 million birders in the United States alone. This study also discovered that one out of every six adults in the United States watches or feeds birds.

Unlike many other hobbies, birding has a unique power to attract people of all ages, backgrounds, and localities. Birds are found everywhere, and many species can be easily identified with little training or experience. It is therefore relatively easy to begin this hobby, but there are endless opportunities to refine and expand one's knowledge and skills.

▼ A trip to a local park or pond is one of the best and easiest ways to get close to wild birds. Many species find food and shelter in urban green spaces.

LET'S INVESTIGATE

BRINGING BIRDS CLOSER

While many birds are often in plain view, flitting about in the hedges next to houses or soaring over a field behind a school, locating others requires greater effort. Try the following techniques to bring birds into closer view.

- Imitate a generalized distress call by repeating a *piissshhhh* sound when a bird of interest is skulking in dense vegetation, especially during the nesting season.
- Make a squeaking sound by kissing the back of the hand to attract a bird's attention.
- Find a nice perch in a tree, and be still: many birds will not be disturbed by a nearby presence and will carry on their normal behavior in close view.
- Create a garden with plants that attract birds and set up feeders and water baths to bring birds closer to a house.

Basic Equipment

Beginning birders need three fundamental pieces of equipment to get started: binoculars, an identification guide, and a field notebook. They make it easier to identify more challenging species, to reference identifying characteristics, and to keep notes on observations. Most birders compile a checklist of species they have seen and make notes about birds they were not able to identify in the field. They can go back to their records later and try to figure out what they have seen.

Binoculars and Scopes

The most important piece of gear for birders of any level is suitable binoculars to magnify a bird and allow a close-up view. Although some birds can be easily identified without the use of binoculars by someone with a basic understanding of their shape, size, behavior, and location, binoculars are essential for identifying many other species. Binoculars also make observing birds more enjoyable, because they enable the viewer to see the beautiful details in plumage patterns and colors, bill shapes, foot structures, and so on. Binoculars are available in an array of

▶ Artificial nest boxes close to houses or in backyards often attract wild birds to breed. They provide excellent opportunities to observe the nesting behavior of parents and young, such as these tree swallows (*Tachycineta bicolor*).

magnification powers, fields of view, lens coatings, sizes, weights, styles, and prices. Birders usually try as many models of binoculars as they can before making a purchase.

The key characteristics of binoculars are the magnification power, field of view, light-gathering capacity, and lens coating. Binoculars are classified by a system consisting of two numbers, such as 7x35, 8x40, 10x40, or 10x50. The first number refers to the magnification power, and the second number refers to the field of view. A magnification power of 8 means that the object viewed will appear eight times its actual size through the lenses. The field-of-view number describes the diameter of the

▼ Knowing where birds will be, and when, is important. These birders are at the southern tip of Spain, where Europe is only a few miles from Africa. Millions of birds pass over this headland as they migrate twice yearly between their breeding and wintering areas.

binoculars' objective lens (the one farthest from the eye) in millimeters and refers to the width of the space seen when looking through the binoculars. The field of view also influences the light-gathering capacity of binoculars. A larger diameter allows more light to enter the optics, making the image appear brighter and colors more vivid in low light conditions, such as during sunrise or sunset or in cloudy or rainy weather. Special coatings applied to the lenses of more expensive binoculars also increase their light-gathering capacity.

Most birders seem to prefer either 8x40 or 10x40 binoculars because they provide sufficient magnification for most conditions and a field of view suitable for finding birds easily in open or dense vegetation. Although binoculars with a higher power of magnification will make a bird appear larger, they also make it harder to hold the image steady.

Many birders also choose to use a spotting scope with greater magnification power than

LET'S INVESTIGATE

IDENTIFYING BIRDS

Successfully identifying many birds requires more than just noting their plumage color and pattern and comparing them to the images in a field guide. Colors and patterns often vary according to gender, age, time of the year, and the amount of normal wear and tear on the feathers. A good birder will take a number of factors into account to make a conclusive identification. Consider the following factors when identifying a bird.

- Analyze its shape. Is it fat or skinny? Does it have a long tail or legs? Note these and any other striking details.
- Estimate its size by comparing it to a familiar bird.
- Observe its posture. Is the bird upright, hunched, or horizontal?
- Observe how the bird flies. Is its flight direct, erratic, undulating, soaring, flapping, or gliding?
- Watch the way it behaves. A bird may climb, hop, run, catch insects from the air, or bob its tail.
- Listen to its song. Birdsong is quite variable, from melodic or complex to rasping, buzzing, or shrieking.
- In what sort of habitat is the bird? Many bird species have a preferred habitat, whether pasture, wetland, forest, or scrub.
- Check the geographic distribution of similar-looking birds in a field guide to discover which species inhabit that particular area.
- Many birds move around and may be found in different places at different times of year. Refer to a field guide to find out which species should be present at that particular season.

binoculars to observe really distant birds or to admire intricate details of a bird at relatively close range. Although spotting scopes are quite a bit more expensive than binoculars, they are particularly useful for helping birders identify and observe waterfowl and shorebirds that live in expansive habitats such as lakes, wetlands, and open fields.

Field Guides

Another essential piece of equipment for birders is a good field identification guide. A typical field guide is a small- to medium-sized book that includes paintings or photographs, distribution maps showing where each species can be found and when, written descriptions of the appearance of each species, descriptions of any aspects of behavior that help to identify it, information about the habitats it frequents, and often a comparison to similar-looking species with which it may be confused. Field guides serve a dual purpose for most birders. Their primary use is to be carried in the field for easy reference to make a species identification on the spot, but they also typically contain detailed information that makes them useful for studying at home before or after a birding field trip.

Field guides are usually arranged to cover all of the species that can be found within a specific geographic region, state, country, or

LET'S INVESTIGATE

KEEPING A FIELD JOURNAL

Taking notes and making sketches in the field can serve as a learning tool, as a reference for further reflection, and as a historical record of birding activities. Recording observations in an organized and standardized format makes them easy to interpret. Important data to record for each journal entry include the owner's name and birding partners, date and time of observation, specific location, weather conditions and habitat, species identified and numbers of individuals, and general notes on behavior and appearance. Use a waterproof pen on good quality paper that will better absorb the ink and that will resist fading or becoming brittle to preserve the records for the longest possible time. One of the most widely used methods of field journaling is the Grinnellian system, developed in the early 20th century by Joseph Grinnell. Try managing checklists and observations or view the notes of other birders by using a free online application, developed at the Cornell Laboratory of Ornithology, called eBird (http://www.ebird.org/content).

continent. For example, you can find field guides that cover all of the birds recorded in North America, or guides that focus specifically on the birds of eastern or western North America. There are a great number of field guides to choose from that cover North American birds. The field guide that works best for any individual birder is really a matter of personal preference. Most birders prefer guides with paintings rather than photographs. The size of the guide is important. Most guides are small enough to fit in a coat pocket. A larger guide may contain more information but may not be practical for carrying in the field.

Audio Guides

Birders often acquire audio guides that help them learn to identify the voices of birds, because many bird species are more often heard than seen, and others are more readily distinguished by the sounds they make than

▶ Visiting nature preserves is an excellent way to see a variety of birds. Preserves are home to many birds, and many have bird blinds for observing birds without being detected.

◀ Birding is always enjoyable in small groups. Everyone gets to see more birds, and the more experienced birders can help beginners find and identify birds.

by their appearance or behavior alone. Audio guides usually include a series of compact discs or digital audio files and an accompanying manual that details the contents and instructs the birder about how to use the guide. Learning to identify birds by sound is an essential skill for successful birding ventures in many parts of the world.

Audio Recording

Many birders become interested in making their own audio recordings of birds in the field as a means to help identify difficult species, create a sound record of their field trip, or even contribute to sound archives that are used by other birders or professional ornithologists to investigate all sorts of scientific questions. Basic audio recording equipment can be quite expensive and

typically consists of a parabolic or shotgun-style microphone, a sound amplification device, and an analog or digital recording unit that creates a permanent copy of the acquired sounds. Anyone interested in recording bird sounds can learn more about sound recording equipment and techniques, listen to a variety of animal sounds, and even sign up for a recording workshop by visiting the Macaulay Library Web site at the Cornell Laboratory of Ornithology (http://www.birds.cornell.edu/macaulaylibrary).

Outdoor Gear

Most birders dress for the field as if they were going on a hike and typically wear a hat to protect them from the sun, rain, or snow, a few removable layers of clothing, and footwear suitable for the expected temperature and terrain. A backpack to carry an identification guide and field notebook, trail map and compass, basic first aid kit, some food, and a bottle of water is a good idea for most field trips. A sturdy pair of hiking boots is suitable and comfortable enough for most conditions and is essential to navigate any steep or slippery terrain. A good raincoat and an extra warm thermal layer are needed if it is cold or there is chance of rain. Birders should carry only what they need to be comfortable in the current conditions, not burdening themselves with any unnecessary equipment, so they can focus on observing birds and enjoying the experience of being outdoors.

For discussion of the scientific study of birds, see:
    Ornithology

Birds of Paradise

Many birds have spectacular plumage, but few can match the dazzling beauty and diversity of the birds of paradise family (Paradisaeidae). Renowned for their iridescent colors, extravagant plumes, and dramatic mating-display rituals, these exotic creatures remain among the most elusive and mysterious of all birds, thanks to the remoteness of their habitats.

Birds of paradise are closely related to the crow family (Corvidae), and many species have a distinctly crowlike look, with sturdy bodies, stout bills, and strong legs and feet. Most authorities recognize 44 species, all classified within a single family, but recent DNA studies suggest that four species are not closely related to the others and should perhaps be classified in separate families.

The Paradisaeidae family includes eight species in which both sexes have similar, relatively drab plumage and breed in monogamous pairs. In all the more flamboyant species, the mature males are polygamous, mating with as many females as possible each season. The males sport an extraordinary variety of plumes, feathery shields, streamers, and pennants in addition to vivid, glittering colors. Despite this visual diversity, however, many of these species are genetically very similar. They may interbreed to produce hybrid forms that were wrongly identified as separate species in the past.

▶ A male Raggiana bird of paradise flaps its wings to reveal its long, gauzy plumes. When erected in full display, the plumes form a glorious fountain of rich, soft color.

Island Forests

Most birds of paradise are restricted to Papua New Guinea, Papua (formerly Irian Jaya), and nearby islands. Four species occur in the tropical forests of northeastern Australia. Although a few frequent mountain woodland, lowland savannas, or coastal mangroves, most species live in the tropical rain forests at various elevations, each with its own altitude range.

Many species feed on a wide variety of foods, including insects, spiders, frogs, and especially fruit. This diverse diet is reflected by the relatively short, strong, general-purpose bills of some species. Other species are

Order Passeriformes

Family Paradisaeidae

Number of genera 17

Number of species 44

Range Papua New Guinea, Papua (Indonesia), and northeastern Australia

Size range Length 6–44 in. (15–111 cm); wingspan 12–25 in. (30–64 cm); weight 1.8–16 oz. (51–454 g)

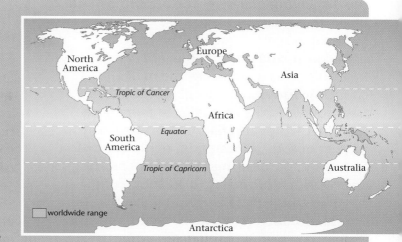

specialized insect eaters with long, slender, curved bills that they use to probe crevices for prey, although they may also eat some fruit.

The monogamous species tend to live at high altitudes, where food can be scarce, and both parents must cooperate to feed their young. At lower altitudes, on the other hand, food is usually abundant. This probably accounts for the evolution of a breeding system in which the female can feed the young alone, while the male devotes his time to feeding himself and displaying his finery.

Dazzling Displays

The males of most monogamous species of birds of paradise do not have to compete so intensively for mates, so they have not evolved particularly elaborate courtship displays. The trumpet manucode (*Manucodia keraudrenii*), for example—a species found in both New Guinea and Australia—confines itself to a short chase and display in the trees, but it does have a specialized syrinx (a bird's vocal apparatus) that enables it to produce a loud, trumpetlike call.

Polygamous males are very different, for every species has its own unique, usually flamboyant display. The smallest species, the king bird of paradise (*Cicinnurus regius*), is

mainly vivid crimson, flushed with orange, and has two tail quills tipped with iridescent green discs. Like many other species, he displays on a designated perch, fluffing out his body feathers and raising his elaborate tail quills above his head. Then he suddenly tips upside down to hang by his feet, his outspread wings vibrating and his bill open to display its bright yellow-green lining.

Other species clear a display ground, or lek, of leaf litter and twigs on the forest floor. One such species is the western parotia (*Parotia sefilata*), which is black with an iridescent golden-green breast shield, silver feathers on its crown, and six long head filaments tipped with tiny black pennants. Having prepared his stage, the male dances from side to side while holding a ruff of black plumage out like a ballerina's tutu. At the climax of the dance, he shakes his silver-crowned head from side to side like a limbo dancer, so fast that the crown of long quills is often reduced to a blur.

The females watch these displays, moving from one lek to another to compare different males and select the best performer. The most vigorous, impressive, and therefore fittest male gets to mate with most of the available females. Only a small percentage of the displaying males get the opportunity to breed each year.

In some species, such as the Raggiana (*Paradisaea raggiana*) and blue (*Paradisaea rudolphi*) birds of paradise, the males cooperate in group performances on traditional display trees: ten or more birds flap their wings and flaunt their luxuriant plumes of soft, shimmering, richly colored feathers while uttering raucous or crackling cries. The males display to each other as much as to the females, to establish a dominance hierarchy and to secure the best display perches. When females arrive, rival males display with extra intensity, but the spectators nearly always choose to mate with the dominant, or alpha, male.

Concealed Nests

After mating with females, only the males of monogamous species play any further part in breeding. The females of most birds of

REPRODUCTION AND HEREDITY

SEXUAL SELECTION

Evolution is typically driven by natural selection—the "survival of the fittest"—in the struggle to reproduce. In the polygamous birds of paradise, however, the evolution of the males' plumage has been largely directed by the sexual selection exercised by the females. Since most females choose to breed with the most spectacular males, these individuals father more young, while the genes of less fit males are not passed on to future generations. A comparatively drab male may be perfectly fit for survival, but if he does not breed, his genetic line becomes extinct. This helps explain why these birds of paradise have evolved an astonishing diversity of plumage while remaining genetically very similar.

paradise nest alone, and the males have no contact with their young. The breeding details of some species have never been recorded, but typically they nest in trees, using orchid stems, mosses, and fern fronds to build open, cup-shaped nests in well-concealed sites, laying one or two pink to buff eggs with darker streaks.

The female Raggiana bird of paradise incubates her eggs for 18 to 20 days. She then feeds the young for another three weeks, initially on insects but increasingly with fruit. At the end of this period, the nestlings of both sexes fledge into drab, female-type plumage. The young males may

◀ Deep in the forests of Papua, Indonesia, a western parotia approaches the climax of the ritual display dance that may win him a chance to mate.

▼ A tribesman in the highlands of New Guinea flaunts a magnificent ceremonial headdress made from the plumes of parrots and birds of paradise.

BIRDS AND HUMANS

HUNTING FOR PLUMES

The native peoples of New Guinea have hunted birds of paradise for their glorious plumes for thousands of years, and the feathers are an integral part of many ceremonial headdresses and rituals. In the 19th century, however, they also became a fashionable addition to ladies' hats in Europe and the United States, and their high commercial value led to a big increase in hunting. Eventually all such commercial hunting was banned, and in Papua New Guinea it is now illegal for nonnationals to possess either a live bird of paradise or its feathers. Local tribespeople are permitted to catch the birds for their plumes, but only on a small, sustainable scale.

retain this plumage for six years or more. They attain their full feathered glory only when the influence of the older males in the area has waned and the younger birds have some chance of mating.

Deforestation Threat

The tropical forests of New Guinea are still a largely unspoiled wilderness, and the habitats of most birds of paradise are still intact. Some areas are under threat, either because of

logging, or clearance for agriculture or mining. As a result, seven species are classified as "near threatened" by the World Conservation Union (IUCN). Another three species are in more serious trouble and are classified as "vulnerable." Currently, however, none are seriously endangered, and conservation efforts may yet reverse the fortunes of those species that are under pressure.

SEE ALSO

Courtship and Mating • Displays • Feathers and Plumage • Passerines • Sexual Differentiation

Margaret E. Heggan Free Public Library
208 East Holly Avenue
Hurffville, New Jersey 08080

Birds of Prey

Few birds are quite so exciting as birds of prey. Others may be beautiful or fascinating, but birds of prey are thrilling. There is something about a hunter that stirs the imagination. One may pity its victims yet marvel at the skill and power of the predator. Catching prey can be difficult and dangerous and makes huge demands of the physical abilities of the hunter. Birds of prey have evolved into superbly efficient creatures, capable of astonishing feats of speed, strength, and aerial agility. They are also relatively scarce, simply because it takes a lot of prey animals to support a single hunter. To see one at all is unusual, and to see one in action is rare.

What is a bird of prey? There are many types of hunting birds, including shrikes, owls, and even swifts and tyrant flycatchers. Some may hunt only tiny insects, but they are still predators that prey on other animals. They are not all birds of prey, however. This term covers only those closely related species with powerful talons and hooked bills that

▼ Patrolling low over the ground with the slow, buoyant flight typical of its kind, this male northern harrier has seized a small bird in its sharp talons.

Order Falconiformes

Families Cathartidae, Pandionidae, Accipitridae, Sagittariidae, Falconidae

Number of genera 81

Number of species 313

Range Worldwide except Antarctica and a few oceanic islands

Size range Length 6–60 in. (15–152 cm); wingspan 1–10 ft. (30 cm–3 m); weight 1.1 oz.–31 lb. (31 g–14 kg)

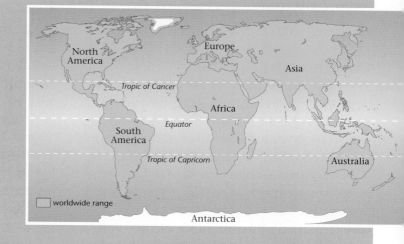

hunt by day, such as the hawks, kites, eagles, and falcons, as well as vultures. An owl is a hunter, but it is not technically a bird of prey, mainly because it has completely different evolutionary history. Neither is a shrike, even though shrikes have hooked bills and frequently kill small birds, mice, and lizards. The tiny Philippine falconet (*Microhierax erythrogonys*), however, which feeds almost exclusively on insects, is definitely a bird of prey. A falconet may be no bigger than a sparrow, but it is a close relative of more formidable hunters like the peregrine falcon (*Falco peregrinus*), one of the most devastatingly effective predators on the planet.

Birds of prey are also known as *raptors*, a term that means "plunderer," like a bandit or pirate. The word certainly sums up their relationship with other animals. It is also appropriate for vultures, which specialize in scavenging the remains of dead animals. Vultures very rarely kill their own prey and are not well equipped for doing so, yet they are still considered as birds of prey because some of them are closely related to hawks and eagles. Vultures are not the only birds of prey that make a living from scavenging. Several other raptors prefer to leave the hard

▼ The bateleur (*Terathopius ecaudatus*) of the African savannas is a snake-eating eagle. Its French name means "tumbler," and refers to the species' acrobatic courtship displays.

work of hunting to other species. Even some powerful eagles and falcons will take advantage of free food if they get the chance.

Families and Habitats

The majority of birds of prey belong to the large and diverse family Accipitridae. The 240 species in this family include kites such as the swallow-tailed kite (*Elanoides forficatus*), harriers like the northern, or hen, harrier (*Circus cyaneus*), forest hawks such as the northern goshawk (*Accipiter gentilis*), and buteos like the red-tailed hawk (*Buteo jamaicensis*). The family also includes all the eagles—fish eagles like the bald eagle (*Haliaeetus leucocephalus*), snake eagles such as the African bateleur, and booted eagles like the golden eagle (*Aquila chrysaetos*)—as well as the Old World vultures of Africa and Asia. The seven species of American New World vultures are classified in a family of their own, the Cathartidae, because certain evidence suggests that they are not closely related to the other birds of prey.

The second largest family is the Falconidae, which includes 64 species. Most of these are typical falcons of the genus *Falco*, such as the peregrine falcon, the prairie falcon (*Falco mexicanus*), and the kestrels. The family also includes the very small pygmy falcons and falconets, the forest falcons and laughing falcon (*Herpetotheres cachinnans*) of the American tropics, and the caracaras of Mexico and Central and South America. Two birds of prey species with particularly unusual features and no close living relatives are classified in families of their own—the osprey in the Pandionidae, and the secretary bird in the Sagittariidae.

The species in these various families encompass a wide variety of size, form, diet, and behavior and have been able to colonize most of the habitats on Earth, apart from the permanent ice sheets and open oceans. Some, like the gyrfalcon (*Falco rusticolus*), are Arctic specialists, while others, like the American harpy eagle (*Harpia harpyja*), are found only in lowland tropical forests. The snail kite

▲ The tiny African pygmy falcon (*Polihierax semitorquatus*) is the size of a starling, yet it regularly preys on other small birds, lizards, and rodents, as well as insects.

(*Rostrhamus sociabilis*) is restricted to marshlands and swamps, while the Afro-Asian lappet-faced vulture (*Torgos tracheliotus*) ranges over arid deserts. Some species, like the Hawaiian hawk (*Buteo solitarius*) and the Mauritius kestrel (*Falco punctatus*), are restricted to isolated oceanic islands, while others, like the peregrine falcon and osprey, occur almost worldwide.

Butcher Bills

Nearly all birds of prey are instantly recognizable as such because they share a number of key features that make them effective hunters and meat eaters. The most obvious of these is the sharp, hooked bill. This bill looks like a deadly weapon, but for most birds of prey it is strictly a butcher's tool, used for ripping away skin, fur, and feathers and stripping meat from bones. A big vulture can use its heavy bill to slice through cowhide, and many smaller scavengers often rely on the biggest vultures to do this job for them.

The bill is also a precision tool, enabling a nesting eagle to present her newly hatched nestlings with delicate morsels of meat that they can swallow easily. The highly specialized snail kite of the American tropics and Florida Everglades employs the extended, bladelike hook of its bill like a scalpel. It probes into the shell of an aquatic snail, locates the muscle attaching the animal to its shell lining, and severs it with surgical accuracy.

Some birds of prey also use their bills to kill their victims. Snake eagles, for example, specialize in eating snakes that may be armed with powerful venom and that have to be immobilized quickly. A snake eagle often holds down a snake with its feet while rapidly biting it behind the head to sever the spinal cord. Achieving this is no easy feat, however. The European short-toed eagle (*Circaetus gallicus*) often has to engage the snake in a deadly dance—each trying to outwit the other—before it can deliver its fatal blow.

▲ The formidable talons of a bird of prey can crush the life from a small animal or impale some vital organ. Only falcons regularly use their hooked bills to kill their prey.

Deadly Talons

The main weapons of most birds of prey are their feet, which have powerful talons. They have relatively short toes for strength and sharp, sturdy, curved claws for piercing the bodies of their victims. When an eagle seizes a rabbit, for example, it generally kills it instantly as its claws close together and damage some vital organ. Even if nothing major is damaged, the force of impact is often fatal.

As with songbirds, the three forward-pointing toes are balanced by a fourth that points backward. On birds of prey, this toe is generally armed with a particularly long, sharp claw that makes an effective dagger. The peregrine falcon can use this claw to strike its prey dead in midair. Many species, such as the merlin (*Falco columbarius*), have extra-long legs that give them an extended reach. The talons are also used to carry the prey to a feeding perch or back to the nest.

All this use puts enormous stress on the bird's legs and feet, which have to be a lot stronger than those of most other birds. The

▲ A falcon's short, hooked bill is specially equipped for killing prey. A falcon has a small, toothlike projection halfway along the upper part of its bill that can be inserted between the individual spinal bones of small animals to sever the spinal cord.

BIRDS AND HUMANS

FALCONRY

Popular for at least four thousand years, the sport of falconry is still practiced by around twenty thousand falconers worldwide. The birds—which include hawks and eagles as well as falcons—are allowed to fly free in pursuit of game and are trained to return to the wrist of the falconer. They can escape if they want to, so they are usually well treated.

Falconry creates a demand for young birds of prey, which encourages poachers to take them from the wild. This act is illegal, but since the thieves can get a huge price for a prized bird such as a peregrine falcon, they are prepared to take the risk. Despite strict protection, many peregrine pairs have their young stolen each year.

▲ Although some birds of prey used for falconry are taken illegally from the wild, most are bred in captivity from parents that may themselves be captive bred.

feet of the American harpy eagle are so strong that it can swoop down to seize a monkey or sloth that is clinging to a tree, rip it from its branch, and fly off with it. The elastic tendons in the legs also work like shock absorbers to prevent bone fractures when the flying bird strikes its prey. The lower legs are covered by tough scales to protect them from victims that may fight back. Those of the booted eagles and some other species are further protected by feathers that extend right down to the feet.

Unlike other birds of prey, the carrion-feeding vultures have relatively weak legs and feet, with long toes and flattened claws. Since they do not have to kill their prey, they do not need to use their feet as weapons. They do not even use them to ferry meat back to the nest, since they feed their young by swallowing food and regurgitating it later on demand.

Eagle Eyes

Catching and killing prey are essential skills, but first the birds must locate it. For a few species this is easy, because their preferred food is abundant, concentrated, and easy to find. For most, however, it is a case of searching over a relatively wide area for

▶ The large, sensitive eyes of Cooper's hawk (*Accipiter cooperii*) enable it to detect the slightest movement in the forest and spring an ambush of deadly accuracy.

elusive creatures that scatter or dive into cover at the first sign of danger.

The main strengths of birds of prey are their acute eyesight and their flying skills. Nearly all hunt by day, so vision is their primary sense. The eyes of a hawk are justly famous; they are far more sensitive than a human's. The retina of an eagle's eye may be as large as that of a human's, but it has roughly five times the number of sensory cells that register shape and movement. These attributes increase its resolution fivefold. The bird can therefore see a far greater amount of detail and can detect movement at long range. A human might perceive a flicker of movement in the grass from across the highway, but a hawk could detect it from a distance of a mile (1.6 km) or more.

A hawk's eyes also have a built-in zoom function. One part of the retina—the fovea— has a particularly dense concentration of sensory cells. By instinctively centering its target on the fovea, the bird can render it in even greater detail. Since its eyes face forward, it can focus in this manner with both eyes at the same time to get a high-definition image, almost like using a pair of powerful binoculars. It is therefore able to locate and assess prey at a distance and can accurately judge its range as it swoops in for the kill.

Sounds and Smells
Hearing also plays a part. The ears of a bird of prey are not as sensitive as those of an owl, which are among the most efficient in the animal kingdom, but they are still far better than human ears. A northern harrier hunting from a perch overlooking a patch of rough grassland will often hear the rustle of a potential meal before it sees the twitch of grass that betrays its location.

Some New World vultures also rely on their sense of smell to locate food. Most birds—and all other raptors—have a poorly developed sense of smell, but experiments have shown that turkey vultures (*Cathartes aura*), in particular, often find their meals by detecting the taint of death in the air. Black vultures (*Coragyps atratus*) and condors do not seem to share this high degree of scent perception, so the turkey vulture's finely tuned sense of smell may be unique.

Soaring and Gliding
The acute senses of birds of prey enable them to locate food, but they also rely heavily on their flying skills when searching for prey or mounting an attack. Many range over huge territories, staying airborne for

hours, and most species depend on speed and maneuverability to catch their quarry. The way they fly depends on what they eat and where they live.

Vultures specialize in finding and eating carrion. Sometimes this is the remains of animals that have been dead for some days and are starting to decay, but frequently it is the freshly killed victims of powerful predators such as lions and wild dogs. Many vultures live in mountainous regions, or in open country such as the African savanna grasslands, and they find food by flying high overhead and watching the ground and the activities of other animals.

▼ Although the secretary bird hunts on the ground, it nests in flat-topped trees such as the spiny acacias that dot the African plains. Here, a pair of secretary birds surveys a possible site.

REGULATION AND BEHAVIOR

THE SECRETARY BIRD

The strangest of all birds of prey is the peculiar secretary bird (*Sagittarius serpentarius*), which is classified in its own family. It gets its name from the quills that seem to be tucked behind its ears, after the habit of 19th-century clerks or secretaries, but its most striking features are its astonishingly long legs. It strides across the African plains like an ostrich, searching for prey such as beetles, mice, lizards, and snakes, and it often kills venomous snakes by stamping on them. It is attracted to grass fires, where it seizes animals escaping from the flames. Despite its preference for hunting on foot, the secretary bird is a graceful flyer, able to soar high in the air like an eagle and to put on a spectacular aerial display during courtship.

ADAPTATION AND DIVERSITY

CONVERGENT EVOLUTION IN VULTURES

With their naked heads, big bills, broad wings, and soaring flight, most vultures are instantly recognizable, yet the American New World vultures are not closely related to the Old World vultures of Africa and Asia. Analysis of their DNA shows that New World vultures, such as the species of New World condors and the turkey vulture, are the closest living relatives of the storks. The Old World vultures share common ancestry with snake eagles. The fact that Old and New World vultures all look much the same is because they have evolved to fill similar ecological niches: soaring high in the air to search for food, then ripping into carrion with their heavy, hooked bills. Their naked heads enable them to probe deep into carcasses without getting their plumage matted with blood. These distantly related groups of vultures represent an example of convergent evolution, in which species with completely divergent origins evolve similar traits, or characteristics, because they share the same way of life.

▼ A zebra carcass attracts a jostling crowd of Rueppell's griffon vultures (*Gyps rueppellii*) and white-backed vultures (*Gyps africanus*) on the grasslands of Tanzania.

To stay in the air without using too much energy, vultures use a technique called soaring, which involves circling and gaining elevation on updrafts without flapping their wings. The updrafts are often caused by rising warm air currents called thermals, but they can also be created by air blowing up over mountain ridges or coastal cliffs. A vulture will frequently circle upward on a thermal, rising higher and higher, then glide out of the rising air and across country, losing height gradually, until it encounters another thermal and soars upward again. It can stay in the air throughout the day with barely a wingbeat. The wings of vultures are perfectly shaped for this style of flight. They are long and broad with splayed feathers at the tips to minimize air turbulence at low speed and improve efficiency.

Buteos and big eagles, such as the golden eagle and African martial eagle (*Polemaetus bellicosus*), use the same technique to search

▲ Cliffs and crags make ideal perches for soaring birds of prey like this Eurasian griffon vulture (*Gyps fulvus*), enabling them to take to the air with minimum effort.

for live prey in open country, but they tend to utilize flapping flight more frequently. A golden eagle, for example, will soar high overhead until it locates a target such as a rabbit, then will approach it prey at low level, flying fast, to ambush it before it can dive into a burrow. The eagle is capable of both soaring and fast direct flight.

Ambush and Pursuit

Many other birds of prey rarely or never soar, preferring to either patrol at low level or hunt from perches. Harriers fly low and slowly over open grassland or marshes, listening for prey and pouncing on any likely victims that they find. Fish eaters like the osprey sometimes hover briefly over water before plunging

▲ The Eurasian kestrel (*Falco tinnunculus*) has perfected the art of hovering, often hanging in the same spot for several minutes as it watches for prey on the ground below.

down to seize fish that have ventured close to the surface. The hovering technique has been perfected by the kestrels and some kites, which are able to "perch" in the sky as if suspended by an invisible thread while they survey the ground below.

Hovering uses a lot of energy, however, and where possible, kestrels and many other birds of prey prefer to hunt from prominent perches that provide clear vantage points over good hunting country. Other species prefer to stay hidden and attempt taking their victims by surprise. In woodlands, forest hawks, like the sharp-shinned hawk (*Accipiter striatus*) and northern goshawk, lurk in ambush, waiting for smaller birds to fly past, before launching themselves in pursuit, dodging and weaving through the trees with deadly agility. These forest hawks of the genus *Accipiter* have relatively shorter wings and longer tails than most birds of prey, giving them the extra maneuverability that they need to chase prey through dense woods.

Some of the most spectacular hunters, however, are the falcons that hunt other birds and insects in the open sky. Their pointed wings are perfectly shaped for speed with extra-long outer flight feathers to provide maximum thrust. They include the merlin, a miniature specialist in high-speed pursuit

that chases small songbirds low over open ground before rising above them to strike. Even faster is the Eurasian hobby (*Falco subbuteo*), which darts after dragonflies, zigzagging through the sky to keep up with their virtually instant changes of direction. The Eurasian hobby is even fast enough to overtake and kill a swift. Most impressive of all is the peregrine falcon, a burly, powerful flyer that patrols high in the sky. It singles out an airborne victim such as a pigeon or duck, then dives in a high-speed "stoop" to collide with its target at shattering speeds of 100 miles (160 km) per hour or more.

Generalists and Specialists

In general, birds of prey hunt animals that are appropriate to their size. The tiny falconets of the genus *Microhierax* prey mainly on flying insects, snatching them out of the air like many tyrant flycatchers do. At the other extreme, the mighty wedge-tailed eagle (*Aquila audax*) of Australia has been known to carry off young kangaroos, but even some big birds of prey will take insects

STRUCTURE AND FUNCTION

THE OSPREY

At first sight, the osprey (*Pandion haliaetus*) looks like a typical bird of prey, yet it is classified in its own family, the Pandionidae, because it has no close living relatives and has evolved a unique combination of characteristics more suitable for capturing and handling fish. Other birds of prey are able to catch fish, but the osprey is a specialist. It has oily, water-resistant plumage that helps it plunge underwater to seize a victim, return to the surface, and fly off again without absorbing much water in its feathers. It can also close its nostrils as it dives, preventing water from being forced into its lungs. Its very strong feet have reversible outer toes and long, curved talons to hook powerful fish, and the soles of its feet are covered with sharp, spiny scales to penetrate fish slime and to give a secure grip on its slippery catch. All of these traits make the osprey such an effective fish predator that it has managed to spread all around the world.

▶ An unwary fish swimming near the surface has made an easy target for this osprey. As it flies off, it carries its catch headfirst to reduce wind resistance.

▲ Widespread in South America, the snail kite also has a small population in the Florida Everglades. This juvenile has caught a snail, its main prey.

and other small animals if they are easy to catch. Many will consume carrion if it is available, as well as other scraps of refuse. For example, the black kite (*Milvus migrans*) of Europe, Asia, Africa, and Australia often feeds in and around towns, picking up edible garbage from city dumps and gutters and even swooping down to snatch food from open-air markets. The caracara species of Central and South America often feed in much the same way. Such birds are called generalists and are opportunistic eaters, ready to try anything once. Such flexible eating habits and broad diets have helped generalists become geographically widespread among different types of habitat.

Many other birds of prey are specialists that focus on one particular type of prey. The most extreme example of a specialist is the snail kite, which targets just one species of

aquatic snail. More dramatically, the bat hawk (*Macheiramphus alcinus*) of Southeast Asia preys mainly on bats, which it snatches at dusk as they leave their daytime roosts in caves. Quite unusually for a bird of prey, it swallows the bats whole. Snake eagles feed almost exclusively on snakes, and the European honey-buzzard (*Pernis apivorus*) digs bees, wasps, and their larvae out of their nests. It carefully snips off the stingers of adult insects before eating them.

Loners and Colonists

A bird's prey often affects its social life. Species that target live mammals and birds tend to hunt alone, or sometimes in pairs, because their prey can be scattered, and there are typically only enough animals in a particular area to support one or two hunters and their young. Species that prey on more abundant insects or other high-density invertebrates, or scavenge from big carcasses, often feed together in groups because there is plenty of food for all.

STRUCTURE AND FUNCTION

SIZE DIFFERENCE
In most birds, the males are either bigger than the females or the same size. In many birds of prey, however, the females are bigger than their mates. In some species, such as the northern goshawk, the female is so much larger than the male that she takes different prey. The reason for this is uncertain, but it seems to be related to the division of labor between the sexes during breeding. It is likely that the female's greater size gives her the extra resources she needs to produce eggs but it also makes her less agile in the air. The lighter, faster male does most of the hunting, while the stronger, more imposing female defends their young.

Most of the lone hunters also roost alone at night and nest in isolated pairs during the breeding season. Each pair has its own exclusive territory, which it defends against other individuals of the same species. This territory is encompassed by a larger home range area that varies in size and exclusivity according to the quality of the habitat and the amount of prey available.

Some essentially solitary hunters, including many kites and harriers, forage alone but retreat to communal roosts at night. Around three hundred harriers of various species were once counted at a single roost in Africa. These species also tend to nest in loose colonies of between five and fifty pairs, with the nests well spaced at intervals of around 230 to 650 feet (70–200 m).

Species that feed together, such as the snail kite, various insect-eating kites and falcons, and the Old World griffon vultures, always form communal roosts and dense nesting colonies. These are often used year after year and can be huge. One roost of insect-eating falcons overwintering in Africa was found to consist of between 50,000 and 100,000 birds. They can live in such densities because there is little competition to feed on the vast swarms of locusts or termites that often plague the tropics.

▼ A lammergeier prepares to drop a bone onto rocks below, to crack it open and reveal the marrow. The birds may use the same bone-cracking sites for many years.

Aerial Displays

The nesting sites used by birds of prey are often occupied for many years or even many generations. The birds return to these historical sites at the beginning of each breeding season. In some species, any males and females that have successfully bred before often meet at their former nest site and pair up again. Their relationship—and

REGULATION AND BEHAVIOR

STRANGE DIETS

Most birds of prey are hunters and scavengers, which feed on the flesh of other vertebrates, such as mammals, birds, reptiles, and fish. A few, however, have distinctly odd diets. The lammergeier (*Gypaetus barbatus*) of southern Europe, Africa, and Asia specializes in eating bones. It swallows them whole to be digested by its highly acidic stomach or drops them from a great height to smash them open and expose the nutritious bone marrow inside. The African grasshopper buzzard (*Butastur rufipennis*) targets grasshoppers and mantises. Strangest of all is the palm-nut vulture (*Gypohierax angolensis*) of tropical Africa, which is largely vegetarian and feeds mainly on the husk of a widely cultivated oil palm fruit.

that of newly established pairs—is often cemented and reinforced by dramatic aerial displays. Both birds swoop up and down through the air and sometimes lock talons and spin earthward before breaking away to repeat the ritual. Male harriers offer food to females who fly up, roll onto their backs, and catch the food in midair.

Once their bond is secure, the birds set about building or repairing a nest. The nature of raptor nests varies enormously, from vast constructions of sticks and branches, in the case of some species like the American bald eagle, to bare ledges in the case of falcons. Some hawks may also take over the abandoned nests of crows or similarly large birds.

Whatever the nature of their nest, birds of prey tend to be very selective about the site. Depending on the species, a nest may be placed on the ground, in a tree, or on a rocky crag or cliff. The peregrine falcon may even nest on a ledge near the top of a tall building.

▼ Like all birds of prey, the crested caracara (*Caracara cheriway*) is an attentive parent, carefully slicing food into small morsels suitable for its down-covered young.

Often there is no shortage of suitable nest sites, but in habitats such as open prairies and savannas, there may be very few, especially for big eagles that nest in tall trees. In these areas, the breeding population is often limited by the number of suitable nesting sites rather than the availability of prey.

Family Responsibilities

Once the nest is ready and the eggs are laid, the males and females of most birds of prey take on very different roles. The female takes responsibility for incubating the eggs, keeping the young warm, and initially feeding them small pieces of food. The male becomes the provider, hunting for the entire family and visiting the nest only to deliver food. Harriers bring food by using the same aerial pass that they practice during courtship, in which the female flies up from the nest to collect her mate's offerings. In most species, however, the male carries the food to the nest in his talons, drops it, and flies off to find more. The female eats what she needs and tears up the rest to feed her young.

The nestlings are well developed when they hatch and are able to see clearly. Gradually they learn how to tear up their

▲ When the young fledge, they grow juvenile plumage that is often quite unlike that of their parents, as with these young black-shouldered kites (*Elanus caerulens*).

own food, and eventually the female is able to leave them alone in the nest and go hunting herself. This relieves some pressure on the male, who no longer has to hunt alone for the whole family, and helps ensure that the growing young get enough to eat as their appetites steadily increase. Eventually the young birds grow their flight feathers and are able to make their first flights. They leave the nest but typically roost nearby while their parents continue to bring them food. By degrees they learn to hunt for themselves and eventually become more or less independent.

Among large birds of prey such as eagles, it may be several years before the young gain their full adult plumage, disperse to a new territory, and breed for the first time themselves. An American bald eagle may not breed until it is five years old, but it has a

REGULATION AND BEHAVIOR

MURDEROUS CHICKS

Many birds of prey, particularly eagles, lay two or three eggs each season but rarely rear more than one nestling successfully. The eggs are laid at two-day or three-day intervals and incubated immediately, so one chick always hatches first. This older, stronger chick takes most of the food brought back to the nest; in some species, it will even kill and eat its siblings. If the first to hatch is not the strongest because of some defect, then the second will be dominant. The situation seems harsh, but it gives the strongest chick a better chance of survival than if all the young shared the food equally. It is more advantageous for parenting birds to rear one healthy chick than two or three weak ones, which might all die.

BIRDS AND HUMANS

PESTICIDE POISONING

In the 1960s and 1970s, many birds of prey came close to extinction from the widespread use of toxic agricultural pesticides. The problem was caused by organochlorine insecticides such as DDT, which were put on many crops to kill insect pests. Seed-eating birds such as pigeons were not affected, but since organochlorines take a very long time to break down, the birds started accumulating DDT in their bodies. As the pesticides washed into waterways, the same thing happened to fish.

A pigeon can accumulate the DDT from 1,000 seeds and not be adversely affected, but if a bird of prey eats 100 contaminated pigeons, it accumulates the DDT of 100,000 seeds. DDT poisoning has the effect of making the predator's eggs more fragile, so they are inadvertently crushed during incubation. Unable to breed and weakened by poison, many species, such as the peregrine falcon and osprey, began to disappear. Almost the entire peregrine population of the eastern United States was destroyed. Eventually organochlorine pesticides were banned in North America and Europe, and birds of prey populations have since recovered. In some places in the tropics, these chemicals are still used to fight insect-borne diseases like malaria, so pesticide poisoning remains a serious problem in many areas.

◄ The provision of nest boxes on tall buildings has provided peregrine falcons with extra nest sites as they recover from near extinction in regions that were badly affected by pesticide poisoning.

potential life span of up to fifty years. In practice, wild bald eagles rarely live half as long, and smaller birds of prey like the American kestrel (*Falco sparverius*) have a life expectancy of ten years at most.

Threats and Outlook

The lives of many birds of prey are cut short by illegal hunting, trapping, and poisoning. This type of persecution continues, even though most species are now protected by law in many countries.

Throughout the world, birds of prey are sometimes targeted as potential threats to domestic livestock and game. Many do eat game birds, valuable fish, and even lambs and young goats, but they rarely pose a serious threat to the populations of their prey. Predator numbers are limited by the amount of prey available, and the hunter population always declines before their prey does. This delicate natural balance allows the prey population to recover until there are enough to support a greater number of hunters again.

Some birds of prey have managed to thrive despite these threats, but they still face a much greater danger from the destruction of their wild habitats. Throughout the world, wilderness is shrinking as more land is colonized and altered by an ever expanding human population. Forests are cut down, wetlands are drained, and the land is turned into pasture for farm animals, cultivated for crops, or developed for human settlement and recreation. The removal of natural vegetation nearly always has a negative impact on prey numbers and reduces the number of suitable nesting sites. For the most part, only those

birds of prey that live in the most remote areas are reasonably secure, and even these may come under threat if the effects of climate change disrupt the natural balance and diversity of plant and animal species. Predators are the first to suffer when a habitat comes under stress. Although some birds of prey are now doing well, the future of many species is yet uncertain.

SEE ALSO

American Kestrel • Bald Eagle
• California Condor • Red-tailed Hawk
• Turkey Vulture

▼ A full-grown pheasant makes ideal prey for the powerful northern goshawk; targeting valuable game birds, however, puts the northern goshawk at risk of human persecution.

Black-capped Chickadee

Popular and inquisitive, the black-capped chickadee (*Poecile atricapillus*) frequently visits suburban bird feeders. Its black cap inspires half of its name, while the rest is derived from the sound of its call—*chickadee-dee-dee*. The black of its cap, and also of its throat, is offset by white cheeks. Its back is greenish-black, and its underparts are a dull white buff. Its long tail is gray, and its wing feathers have narrow white edges.

The black-capped chickadee is one of the most widespread species of the North American representatives of the family Paridae. It is found from coast to coast across the northern two-thirds of the United States and the southern two-thirds of Canada, extending as far south as northern New Mexico. It is a year-round resident within most of its range, but in colder winters, some northern populations may move south.

The black-capped chickadee flourishes in and around deciduous and mixed woodlands, but it also occurs in agricultural and suburban areas. Trees provide it with nest sites as well as with insects and other food. The black-capped chickadee has become very common in gardens where food is abundant or feeders are maintained, and it will sometimes breed in artificial nest boxes.

▶ In winter, as insect food becomes scarcer, the black-capped chickadee increases its seed and berry intake. It is frequently seen at bird feeders.

Scientific name *Poecile atricapillus*

Order Passeriformes

Family Paridae

Range Across northern two-thirds of the United States and southern two-thirds of Canada

Habitat Deciduous and mixed woodlands, especially forest edges, and suburban areas

Conservation status Common

Length 5–6 in. (12–15 cm)

Wingspan 6–8 in. (15–20 cm)

Weight 0.32–0.49 oz. (9–14 g)

Diet Insects and other invertebrates, berries, and seeds

Nest Moss and other coarse material, lined with softer material such as fur, placed in a cavity or large crevice in dead wood

Eggs Usually 6–8, roundish and white with fine spots, reddish brown at larger end

Young Mainly naked with patches of down when hatched; fledged 14–18 days after hatching

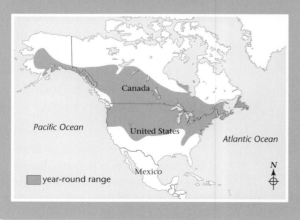

Four-fifths of its diet during the breeding season consists of insects and other invertebrates. Black-capped chickadees move acrobatically through trees, hanging upside down to find insects and their eggs and larvae. They devour many creatures harmful to trees, such as caterpillars, weevils, and sawflies. Every day, an individual chickadee increases its body weight in fat by 10 percent, then loses it again by the end of the night. It has the remarkable ability to reduce its nighttime body temperature—a survival strategy called torpor—from around 108°F to around 88°F (42° to 31°C) to conserve energy.

In late summer and fall, black-capped chickadees cache food to help them through lean periods and can each accurately remember hundreds of hiding places. In winter, they join mixed flocks consisting of several different bird species to forage for food. Seeds and berries form half of their winter diet.

In the early spring, pairs of black-capped chickadees leave the mixed flocks and set up their breeding territories. The female chooses a nest site in a rotten stump or tree, and both birds excavate a cavity for the nest. After the eggs are laid, the male feeds the female, while she incubates the eggs. After hatching between 11 and 13 days later, the nestlings are fed as many as 14 times every hour. They continue to be fed by both parents for up to a month after fledging. In the fall, they join new foraging flocks apart from their parents.

The black-capped chickadee is one of the United States' most common and numerous birds, despite a survival rate of only 30 percent one year after hatching. The provision of high fat and protein foods at suburban bird feeders greatly helps it to survive the winter.

SEE ALSO

Passerines • Titmice and Chickadees • Tufted Titmouse

Blue Jay

Noisy, colorful, and bold, the blue jay (*Cyanocitta cristata*) is a familiar backyard bird throughout much of North America. Like other members of the crow family (Corvidae), the blue jay has a sturdy build and strong bill. Unlike most crows, however, it is vividly colored with a bright blue crest, back, wings, and tail, a black-and-white face, a black collar and nape, off-white underparts, and black, blue, and white bars on its wings and tail. The glorious shades of blue are created by the microscopic structure of the feathers scattering the light, rather than by blue pigments. The same feathers on immature birds are gray rather than blue, and the black plumage has a brown tinge.

The blue jay is widespread east of the Rockies from Texas to southern Alberta and east to Florida and Newfoundland. Birds that breed in the far north in summer migrate south for the winter, usually in loose flocks of five to fifty or more individuals. Many populations that nest farther south are resident throughout the year. It is essentially a bird of mixed woodland, favoring open clearings and woodland fringes, but it has adapted well to suburban and even urban habitats, especially where there are mature oak trees. It is a frequent visitor to backyard feeding stations, especially in winter, and its harsh, piercing cries and rattling whistles are a common feature of many small towns.

The blue jay has an all-purpose bill for dealing with a wide variety of foods. Much of its diet consists of acorns, nuts, and other seeds, which it cracks open on the spot or carries off to store in hidden caches. It also eats many

◀ Resplendent in shades of azure and cobalt blue, a pair of blue jays attend to the needs of their blind, naked, newly hatched young in an apple tree in Ohio.

Scientific name *Cyanocitta cristata*

Order Passeriformes

Family Corvidae

Range United States and southern Canada, east of the Rocky Mountains

Habitat Mixed woodland and suburban gardens

Conservation status Common

Length 10–12 in. (25–30 cm)

Wingspan 13–17 in. (33–43 cm)

Weight 2.5–3.5 oz. (71–99 g)

Diet Acorns, nuts, seeds, fruits, insects, spiders, and small vertebrates

Nest Loose, open cup of twigs and grass, lined with mud and fine, soft rootlets, built in outer branches of a tree, typically 10–30 ft. (3–9 m) above the ground

Eggs 3–6, blue to pale brown, with brown or grey spots

Young Naked, blind, and helpless when first hatched

invertebrates, such as spiders, beetles, bugs, and caterpillars, including the harmful tent caterpillars that swarm in vast numbers in some woodlands and strip the foliage from trees. A pair of blue jays may gather thousands of these caterpillars for their young over the course of the breeding season.

Blue jays also eat many small vertebrates such as mice, frogs, and lizards. They are notorious for robbing the nests of other birds, but eggs and nestlings form a quite small part of their overall diet. In one extensive study of blue jays, only one in a hundred had evidence of eggs or young birds in their stomachs.

Over much of their range, blue jays remain on their breeding territories throughout the year and retain the same partners for life. At the beginning of the breeding season, the male reinforces their relationship with courtship feeding and a sweet warbling song. Pairs often build several nests as part of their courtship ritual. Eventually they chose one nest, complete it, and the female lays her eggs, usually incubating them herself for 16 to 18 days while the male keeps her fed.

Both parents feed the nestlings high-protein foods such as caterpillars and other small invertebrates. At 17 to 21 days old, the young birds' feathers have developed to the degree that they are able to fly, but the parents continue to feed them for another three weeks. The family may stay together until the young are three or four months old. On average, they live for seven years, but some wild blue jays are known to have survived for more than seventeen years.

Blue jay populations are increasing, and the range of the species is expanding westward. Adaptable and intelligent, they are well able to cope with environmental changes, and their future seems secure.

SEE ALSO

American Crow • Crows, Jays, and Magpies • Passerines

Bowerbirds

The bowerbirds of Australia, Papua New Guinea, and Papua (formerly Irian Jaya) are famous for the way the males court their breeding partners by building and decorating bowers designed purely for display and mating. This unusual behavior is unique among birds. The males of many other species attempt to impress females with their nest-building abilities, but only the bowerbirds create special structures that have nothing to do with nesting. In the process, they display such skill and discerning taste that they may well be the most intelligent of all birds.

Bowerbirds were once thought to be closely related to the birds of paradise family, which live in the same region, and were classified together in the same family (Paradisaeidae). Now they are classified in a family of their own and are known to be more closely related to the Australian scrub-bird (Atrichornithidae) and lyrebird (Menuridae) families. Ten of the twenty currently recognized species are restricted to the tropical forests of New Guinea, occurring as high as 13,000 feet (4,000 m) above sea level. Eight other species live only in Australia but occur in a much wider variety of habitats ranging from dry grassland to rain forest. Two species—the fawn-breasted bowerbird (*Chlamydera cerviniventris*) and spotted catbird (*Ailuroedus melanotis*)—occur in both New Guinea and Australia. Some species are widespread, while many others have very restricted ranges.

Contrasting Patterns

The bowerbirds are also rather closely related to the crows and starlings, which they resemble in many ways. They are sturdy, strong-legged birds with quite heavy bills that are well suited to their varied diet. The females are well camouflaged in shades of

▼ A great bowerbird (*Chlamydera nuchalis*) pauses in front of its avenue-style bower, amid a tempting display of red plastic, green broken glass, and white snail shells.

Order Passeriformes

Family Ptilonorhynchidae

Number of genera 7

Number of species 20

Range Australia, Papua New Guinea, and Papua (Indonesia)

Size range Length 8–15 in. (20–38 cm); wingspan 13–23 in. (33–58 cm); weight 2.5–8 oz. (70–230 g)

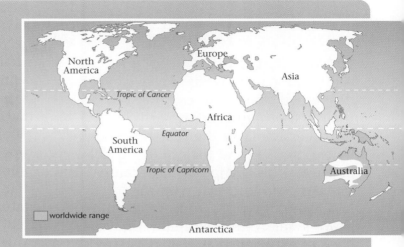

drab brown, gray, or olive, often with some barring or spotting below. The males of many species sport bright, often contrasting patterns of black and brilliant yellow or gold, or have vividly colored crests. Male satin bowerbirds (*Ptilonorhynchus violaceus*) are iridescent blue-black with bright blue eyes. In the four species of catbirds (*Ailuroedus* genus), the sexes are virtually identical, with relatively dull, greenish-brown plumage.

Most bowerbirds feed mainly on fruit, which is available throughout the year in the tropical forests of New Guinea. In more seasonal habitats, they switch to other foods when fruit is not available, taking flowers or seeds, juicy stems, and even leaves—a highly unusual food among all birds. One species, the tooth-billed catbird (*Ailuroedus dentirostris*) of Queensland, Australia, feeds mainly on leaves in winter, chewing them with the aid of two toothlike structures on its upper bill. All bowerbirds will also consume insects, spiders, snails, worms, and similar small invertebrates, as well as some larger animals such as lizards and frogs.

Building Skills

Apart from the catbirds, all male bowerbirds are polygamous, mating with as many females as possible each season. They compete with each other to impress the females, because only those chosen by the females get a chance to breed. This mating system is also characteristic of birds of paradise and jungle fowl like the peacock. In these birds, polygamy has influenced the evolution of spectacular male plumage, as generations of females have selected the most attractive, apparently fittest males. In bowerbirds, it seems that building skills impress females more than fine feathers, so they choose the best bower builders rather than the most handsome males. Since being less conspicuous serves to attract fewer predators, many bowerbird species have evolved relatively subdued male plumage as they have developed their bower-building habit. It is no coincidence that the most elaborate bowers are built by species with the least flamboyant male plumage.

Each species of bowerbird builds a particular form of bower. There are four main types. The simplest is just a roughly circular cleared area or "court," adorned with objects such as leaves or fungi of a particular color. The tooth-billed catbird, for example, favors pale green. More complex is the "mat" built by Archbold's bowerbird (*Archboldia papuensis*)—a carpet of dried ferns and mosses, which the bird gathers together and

REGULATION AND BEHAVIOR

LEARNING CURVE

Although male bowerbirds have a well-developed instinct for creating bowers, their first attempts are quite unsuccessful. Over the years, they learn by experience, and their building skills improve. This is important, because females will mate only with the builders of the most impressive bowers, selecting their mates on the basis of experience as well as innate skill. The females also seem to have individual tastes, and different males of the same species cater to this by offering variations on a basic theme. One may adorn his bower with pink flowers, while another gathers rust-red leaves. Instinct cannot account for such choices, so the birds may have some sort of aesthetic sense.

decorates with black, gray, and blue objects, such as fruits and snail shells.

Nine species build avenue bowers with two parallel walls of sticks or grasses flanking a central avenue that is decorated with colored objects of the birds' choice. The satin bowerbird, for example, favors blue flowers, blue feathers, and even blue plastic bottle tops that match the blue sheen of his plumage. This is also one of several species that paint the walls of their avenues with naturally occurring pigments, using tools held in their bills.

The most elaborate bowers, however, are those built by the Australian golden bowerbird (*Prionodura newtoniana*) and the four gardener bowerbirds (*Amblyornis* genus) of New Guinea. Their "maypole" style bowers are made of sticks arranged around one or more slender tree trunks with a moss lawn at

▼ Adorned with neat piles of richly colored trinkets, the hutlike bower of the Vogelkop bowerbird is perhaps the most sophisticated structure made by any bird.

the base. They range from the relatively simple tower of sticks built by Macgregor's bowerbird (*Amblyornis macgregoriae*) to the astonishing construction of Vogelkop bowerbird (*Amblyornis inornata*), which resembles a small thatched hut.

Dancing Display

Males sing for hours each day by their bowers, using a variety of notes ranging from ringing calls to mechanical rattles and squeaks as well as mimicry of other birds. If a female is attracted to his bower, the male shows it off with a dancing display, often holding one of the colorful ornaments in his bill and calling all the while. If the female is sufficiently impressed—and she will inspect several bowers before making her choice— she allows the male to mate with her.

Apart from the catbirds, which do not build bowers, the males take no further part in raising their young. Each mated female builds her own bulky, cup-shaped nest, usually in the fork of a tree, and lays one or two eggs, which she incubates alone for 19 to

24 days. She also feeds the young during the nestling period, which lasts another 20 days or so. When the young fledge, they all have dull plumage, similar to that of adult females, which makes them difficult to see. In some species, it can take the males up to seven years to attain their full adult plumage and breed for the first time. Females mature at about two years.

Catbirds

Although they are included in the bowerbird family, the four species of catbirds have a quite different breeding strategy. They form monogamous pairs, and the males provide food for the incubating females and help feed the young. Since they do not reproduce by attracting several females, the males have not evolved showy plumage or the ability to build bowers. They do, however, have a distinctive song that sounds much like the mewing of a cat, which accounts for their name.

Highland Wildernesses

Most bowerbirds are fairly secure in their remote habitats. Much of New Guinea, in particular, is still pristine wilderness, but the pressures on its wildlife are increasing all the time. Several species may be threatened by logging, mineral extraction, and the destruction of forest to create farmland. Luckily, many species live in the highlands, where the forces of human destruction are less acute, and most species are classified as being "of least concern" by the World Conservation Union (IUCN).

▼ Despite being closely related to the bowerbirds, the spotted catbird does not build a bower, and the monogamous male looks just like the female.

SEE ALSO
Birds of Paradise • Nests • Passerines

Brown-headed Cowbird

Although it is only a small, dark songbird with few distinctive physical features and a short rising whistle for a song, the brown-headed cowbird (*Molothrus ater*) is one of the most notorious of all North American birds. Its breeding strategy is to lay its eggs in the nests of other birds and to rely on unwitting foster parents to raise its young. In the process, the host bird's own young suffer, mainly through competition with their bigger, stronger cowbird nestlings, and may not survive. As a result, the brown-headed cowbird is widely blamed for population declines in many other American songbirds.

The brown-headed cowbird is one of six species of cowbirds classified in the genus *Molothrus*, five of which have the same breeding system, known to scientists as brood parasitism. Cowbirds are all members of the family Icteridae, the American blackbirds.

Male brown-headed cowbirds are mainly glossy black with an iridescent sheen, and—as the name indicates—a dark brown head, nape, and chest. Females are grayish brown with paler throats and faint streaks on their underparts. They have short, strong, conical bills and dark eyes. Young brown-headed cowbirds of both sexes resemble adult females but are more streaked below.

▼ The back of a bison provides a convenient perch for three brown-headed cowbirds as they pause between feeding forays spent snatching insects disturbed by the animal's feet.

Scientific name *Molothrus ater*

Order Passeriformes

Family Icteridae

Range Throughout United States and Mexico, north to Canada, mainly on grassland

Habitat Mainly grassland with scattered trees, but also farmland and suburbs

Conservation status Common but slowly declining

Length 7–9 in. (18–23 cm)

Wingspan 11–14 in. (28–36 cm)

Weight 1.4–1.8 oz. (40–51 g)

Diet Seeds, insects, and spiders

Nest None; lays eggs in the nests of other birds

Eggs Up to 40 per season, whitish with brown or gray spots

Young Covered with thin gray down when first hatched

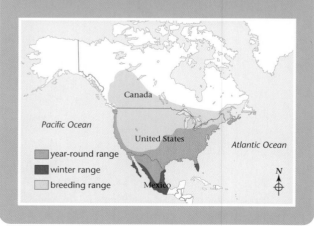

Prairie Nomad

Cowbirds owe their name to their habit of following large grazing animals to seize the insects disturbed by their movements and pick up the seeds that they knock out of the vegetation. Before the 1800s, the brown-headed cowbird was essentially a bird of the Great Plains, where it followed the vast herds of bison that wandered over the prairies. As the human colonists cleared the forests, however, the brown-headed cowbird spread eastward and westward, becoming common across most of North America. It still favors grassland habitats with grazing livestock and low or scattered trees, but it also occurs in suburban areas, where it frequently visits backyard feeding stations.

On the Great Plains, it breeds as far north as the prairies to the west of the Great Slave Lake in northern Canada, but these northern populations migrate south for the winter to the southern United States and Mexico. Some birds winter as far south as southern Florida and southern Mexico. Over much of the United States, brown-headed cowbirds are present throughout the year.

Ground Feeder

The strong, finchlike bill of the brown-headed cowbird is well suited to cracking the tough husks of seeds, which form much of the bird's diet, especially in winter. In spring and summer, it also eats many insects, particularly grasshoppers and beetles, as well as spiders and other small invertebrates. One study of its feeding habits revealed that small animals make up roughly a quarter of its diet.

It locates its food by foraging on the ground, usually around herds of cattle and horses, although it occasionally flies up to snatch slow-flying insects out of the air. It generally walks over the ground as it searches for food, rather than hopping. Outside the breeding season, it frequently feeds in large flocks, often alongside other species of blackbirds, such as the common grackle (*Quiscalus quiscula*).

Brood Parasite

The brown-headed cowbird's habit of following nomadic grazing herds as they ranged across the prairies probably accounts for the evolution of its parasitic breeding strategy. Rarely in the same place for long, it had no time to nest and to raise a family. Instead, it took to laying its eggs in the nests of other birds. It targets a wide variety of species—more than 220 different hosts have been recorded—but favors those that build cup-shaped nests, like the yellow warbler (*Dendroica petechia*). A single female may lay up to forty eggs each season, placing one egg in each nest and often removing one of the host bird's eggs to make room. The cowbird egg is typically larger than the others in the nest and differently colored. Occasionally, the host notices the substitution and destroys it. Usually, however, the bird incubates the cowbird's egg along with its own.

At this point, another important characteristic comes into play. The cowbird egg develops faster than those of its host and hatches first. This ensures that the cowbird nestling is always larger and stronger than its nest mates, enabling it to seize most of the food brought to the nest. The cowbird's ill-fated "siblings" frequently starve as a result, but the intruder will continue to be fed until it is fledged and ready to leave the nest. Many

▼ The unattended nest of a northern cardinal (*Cardinalis cardinalis*) provides a female brown-headed cowbird with an opportunity to lay an egg undetected.

of the small host birds that are parasitized in this way then go on to nest again and attempt to rear another brood. Only the really unlucky ones are targeted by a cowbird a second time.

Steady Decline

During the 1800s and early 1900s, the brown-headed cowbird flourished as a result of the expansion of available habitat. Although the bison herds that it once followed largely disappeared, herds of domestic cattle and other livestock took their place, and the species was able to expand its range and

▲ Despite its mouth lining being red instead of yellow, a cowbird nestling does not arouse the suspicions of this wood thrush (*Hylocichla mustelina*).

numbers considerably. Since the mid-1960s, however, the species has been declining by roughly one percent each year. The reasons are not known but are probably linked to the use of pesticides that eradicate insects and weeds on cropland. Despite this setback, the brown-headed cowbird remains common throughout most of its wide range.

POPULATIONS AND ECOSYSTEMS

COWBIRD CONTROL

Many North American songbird species have suffered sharp population declines in recent decades, and some people believe that brown-headed cowbirds are partly responsible. Since 1800, the species has moved into areas where the local bird populations were not previously exposed to it, and birds such as Kirtland's warbler (*Dendroica kirtlandii*)—an endangered species that nests only in a small area of northern Michigan—have certainly suffered as a result. Two-thirds of Kirtland's warbler nests were being parasitized by cowbirds in the early 1970s. This prompted the U.S. Fish and Wildlife Service to start a cowbird trapping campaign in the region. This intervention may have been one of the reasons the breeding population of Kirtland's warblers doubled between 1972 and 1998. Cowbird control programs on behalf of several other species have not had such clear-cut benefits, however, and it is likely that the main cause of songbird declines is the degradation of their natural habitats by humans.

SEE ALSO

American Blackbirds and Orioles
• Baltimore Oriole • Common Grackle
• Eastern Meadowlark • Passerines
• Red-winged Blackbird

Brown Thrasher

The shy brown thrasher (*Toxostoma rufum*) is more often heard than seen. It may get its name from the way it thrashes around in dead leaves, digging for food, although the word *thrasher* may just be a form of the word *thrush*. The brown thrasher has bright, rusty-brown upper parts, including its long tail. Its pale buff underparts are patterned with parallel black streaks. Each wing has two white bars. The eyes are yellow, and the long beak is slender and curved. Juveniles have dark eyes and less-defined markings than adults.

The brown thrasher is one of the species of the Mimidae family of mockingbirds and thrashers. Its breeding range extends from southern Canada down to eastern Texas, the Gulf Coast, and southern Florida, and west to eastern Colorado. The breeding population north of the southeastern United States migrates south for the winter, while the southern breeders remain resident year-round.

The brown thrasher tends to frequent dense hedgerows and tangled briar patches. It is often found in low shrubs and thorn bushes, where it can hide its nest from egg thieves and escape the attentions of

▼ The male brown thrasher, which sings when courting or warning off intruders, has a larger repertoire of distinct songs than any other bird in North America.

Scientific name *Toxostoma rufum*

Order Passeriformes

Family Mimidae

Range Eastern United States and Canada; northern breeding birds winter in the southern United States

Habitat Dense thickets and hedgerows, and edges of old fields and woods

Conservation status Declining slowly in parts of its range, though still abundant

Length 9–12 in. (23–30 cm)

Wingspan 12.5–14 in. (32–36 cm)

Weight 2.15–3.14 oz. (61–89 g)

Diet Insects, berries, nuts, seeds, worms, snails, and small lizards

Nest Large, mainly twigs, lined with grass, in dense scrub or low in thorny tree, sometimes on ground

Eggs 3–6, pale blue to white, covered with tiny brown speckles

Young Juveniles have dark eyes and less defined markings than adults

predators such as hawks. In urban areas, it favors gardens with mature hedges and thick undergrowth.

Insects, particularly beetles, form a large part of the brown thrasher's diet. It forages for insects in the leaf litter, using its long bill to move twigs, leaves, and small stones, then dig into the ground surface to find grubs and worms. It also eats a great variety of berries, nuts, and seeds.

At the beginning of the breeding season in late March, the brown thrasher is highly visible and audible, as the male, perched high in a tree, loudly sings its songs to attract a female and ward off competitors. The song is easily recognizable—long, variable, melodious, and full of repeated phrases. After mating, both birds build the nest at a site chosen by the female. They take turns incubating the eggs. Hatching takes place between 11 and 14 days. Both adults protect and feed the young until they leave the nest up to 13 days later. Second broods are common, although both the male and female may find new mates for a second nesting attempt, particularly when the first brood has failed.

Brown thrasher populations are still strong, although their numbers have been slowly decreasing in some areas in recent years. This could be due in part to some agricultural practices that remove hedgerows and woodland shelter belts. Natural predators are many, particularly as this bird nests low to the ground, but both birds are ferocious defenders of their nest and can kill snakes and drive off dogs. With an average lifespan of between eight and ten years and with two, or sometimes three, broods a year, the brown thrasher is still far from being endangered.

SEE ALSO

Mockingbirds and Thrashers • Northern Mockingbird • Passerines

Burrowing Owl

Few owls are as distinctive as the burrowing owl (*Athene cunicularia*). Unlike virtually all other owl species, it spends most of its time on the ground, where it can often be seen in broad daylight. It also nests in burrows that have usually been dug by other animals such as ground squirrels. As its name suggests, however, it may excavate its own burrow in suitably soft ground. This behavior is unique among owls, but there are good reasons for it.

Although its habits are unusual, the burrowing owl could never be mistaken for any other type of bird. It has the big, staring, forward-facing eyes typical of owls, with bright yellow irises surrounding the large, dark pupils, accentuated by white eyebrows and a prominent white chin stripe. It has a broad, rounded head and a short, hooked bill. A rather small-bodied owl, it has unusually long, sparsely feathered legs that make it instantly recognizable. Its plumage is sandy brown on the head, back, and upper wings, and creamy white with bold brown spots and streaks on the breast and belly. Females are usually darker than males, and immature birds have pale, unstreaked underparts and dark collars.

The burrowing owl's ground-living and burrowing habits are useful in open grasslands and deserts, where there are very few trees to provide elevated nesting and roosting sites. It will colonize shrubland such as chaparral but avoids areas dominated by mature trees. It also occurs in artificially cleared landscapes such as arable farmland, golf courses, and even airports.

The burrowing owl is widespread in Central and South America, occurring in suitable habitats throughout most of Mexico south to Ecuador and from central Brazil south to Patagonia. In the United States, it occurs throughout the year in the southwestern states from California to Texas, and in summer on the deserts and prairies to the north, as far as southern Canada. In the

◄ Apart from its long, slender legs, the burrowing owl looks like any other owl. It is the bird's ground-dwelling habits that make it so unusual and easy to identify.

Scientific name *Athene cunicularia*

Order Strigiformes

Family Strigidae

Range Southwestern Canada, western United States, Florida, Caribbean islands, Mexico, and Central and South America as far south as Patagonia

Habitat Open grasslands with few trees, and deserts

Conservation status Designated endangered in Canada and of special concern in parts of the United States

Length 8–11 in. (20–28 cm)

Wingspan 20–24 in. (51–61 cm)

Weight 6–7.5 oz. (170–213 g)

Diet Mainly insects and small mammals, birds, and lizards

Nest In burrows that have been abandoned by other animals or that it has excavated itself

Eggs 4–10, white

Young Blind and helpless when hatched, covered in grayish-white down

fall, these northern birds migrate south for the winter. A darker race lives in Florida and on several Caribbean islands.

Varied Prey

Burrowing owls feed mainly on insects and small mammals, varying their prey with the time of year. They take rodents such as mice, gophers, and ground squirrels, as well as lizards, scorpions, and small birds. They are particularly fond of grasshoppers and beetles, which they often pursue over the ground on foot. They will also search for prey from the air, often hovering briefly to pinpoint a target. If a high perch such as a fence post or pole is available, a burrowing owl will use it as a vantage point, watching the ground keenly for any movement, then gliding down to strike. It may also use its talons to catch flying insects in midair.

Since these owls locate their prey mainly by sight, they hunt primarily at dawn and dusk, when nocturnal animals are active but visible. They will hunt at night, however, and even throughout the day in the breeding season when they are feeding young. When they are not hunting, they tend to perch near their burrow entrances, frequently on one foot, blinking in the sunlight. They are often bold and approachable, but when they are feeling threatened, they bob their bodies up and down while giving a harsh rattle of alarm. If a burrowing owl gets seriously alarmed, it adopts a characteristic defensive posture with its head lowered, eyes blazing, and wings partly fanned out to make itself look bigger and more imposing.

Aerial Displays

The breeding season varies greatly among burrowing owl populations, partly because the owl occurs from the Canadian prairies to the tropics and partly because its large range also extends well into the Southern Hemisphere, where the seasons are reversed. On the North American grasslands, the season begins in March or April, at which time the males start displaying to potential mates. They perform aerial displays, rising quickly to 100 feet (30 m) or so, hovering for a few seconds, then dropping 50 feet (15 m) or more before flying up again, repeating the performance several times. They also display on the ground, flashing their white plumage patches and giving a mellow, cooing *toot tooo* territorial song.

The territory is centered on the burrow. This is typically an abandoned ground squirrel or badger hole, but in sandy ground the owls may dig their own, using their bills as well as their long legs. They often nest in loose colonies, probably not because they are particularly sociable, but because the burrows they often adopt have been dug by colonial animals such as prairie dogs. Each nesting burrow is associated with at least one other

▼ Sticking close to their mother, two young burrowing owls emerge cautiously from their nursery burrow in South Dakota.

POPULATIONS AND ECOSYSTEMS

PRAIRIE PARTNERS
In North America, the biggest populations of burrowing owls are associated with colonies of the burrowing ground squirrels known as prairie dogs. Before the prairies were colonized by farmers and ranchers, around 5.5 billion prairie dogs lived across the Midwest in vast colonies known as prairie dog towns. Some of these colonies were immense networks of tunnels, covering huge areas. One found on the high plains of Texas in about 1900 was as big as Lake Michigan. Such colonies offered plenty of nesting holes for burrowing owls, and the paririe dogs' disappearance over the years is one of the main reasons for the owl's decline.

▶ This gecko (a type of lizard) is typical of the type of prey taken by burrowing owls. The owls often hunt by day and night, especially when they are feeding young.

burrow, which is used as a roosting site by the male while the female incubates the eggs.

Eggs are laid from mid-May to early June on the northern prairies. Each female lays six to nine eggs, or sometimes more, at daily intervals and starts their 28-day incubation immediately after the first one is laid. This results in hatching at daily intervals, and the youngest, smallest chicks may not survive if food runs short. The male brings food for the incubating female and for the chicks when they hatch.

Both parents guard the young against ground predators such as badgers and skunks, but the owlets are not entirely reliant on their parents' protection since they can give a very good imitation of a rattlesnake's warning rattle to deter intruders. After about two weeks, they appear above ground and can often be seen at the burrow entrance waiting for the adults to return with food. They leave the nest altogether at about 44 days old to roost in nearby burrows, and they begin hunting insects a week or two later.

Disappearing Habitats

Like many animals of the open grasslands, burrowing owls have suffered from loss of their wild habitats. They are reasonably secure in some of the more remote regions of Central and South America, but in much of North America, vast tracts of prairie have been plowed for growing crops, evicting the burrowing rodents that the owls often rely on to dig their nesting holes. The birds also find a lot less to eat on farmland, particularly where pesticides are routinely used.

As a result, many burrowing owl populations are in decline. The owls have virtually disappeared from North Dakota and western Montana, and in Canada their numbers have dropped by more than half in just ten years. The World Conservation Union (IUCN) considers the species to be endangered in Canada and a "species of special concern" in several American states. The burrowing owl is protected under legislation that makes killing the birds and destroying their nests illegal, but this does not prevent the gradual erosion of their habitat. Eventually they may be confined to the driest grasslands and deserts and will disappear from the prairies altogether.

SEE ALSO

Barn Owl • Elf Owl • Great Horned Owl • Owls

Cactus Wren

Active, inquisitive, and with a habit of perching in full view while singing its harsh, repetitive song, the cactus wren (*Campylorhynchus brunneicapillus*) is a prominent part of the wildlife in the deserts of the Southwest. It is bigger and more striking than most wrens, with a sharp, curved bill and a relatively long tail. It has a conspicuous white stripe over its eye, a dark brown crown, and a paler brown back with white streaks. Its wings and tail are heavily barred with black, buff, and white, and its pale breast is densely spotted with black. The sexes look alike. A juvenile has a darker crown and a paler, more sparsely spotted breast. The markings on its back and wings are also paler.

This bird is well named, as cacti are central to its way of life. It lives only in the cactus deserts of the southwestern United States and northern Mexico, and it is restricted to areas where large cacti grow. It typically nests among the spines of a cactus plant—to take some advantage from the protection they provide against predators. This species may sometimes even eat cactus fruits.

Despite this occasional taste for fruit, however, the cactus wren is essentially an insectivore. It searches for beetles, flies, grasshoppers, ants, wasps, and small spiders, using its sharp, moderately long bill to probe crevices in tree bark and turn stones and dead leaves on the ground. It may also consume small frogs or lizards and eat a few seeds.

▶ The succulent fruit of a giant saguaro cactus may tempt a cactus wren away from its usual diet of insects, spiders, and other small animals.

It forages mainly in the early morning before the desert sun gets too hot, retreating into the shade toward noon and emerging again when the heat of the day is over. It therefore avoids losing too much vital body moisture, enabling it to survive on just the water absorbed from its food. It often forages near human settlements, where it is surprisingly bold in its behavior, entering porches and sometimes cars looking for prey.

Cactus wrens defend territories throughout the year, favoring a spot among cactus scrub

Scientific name *Campylorhynchus brunneicapillus*

Order Passeriformes

Family Troglodytidae

Range Southwestern United States from southern California to southern Texas, and northern Mexico

Habitat Arid and semi-arid desert with cacti and thorn scrub, mainly below 4,000 ft. (1,200 m), but up to 6,000 ft. (1,800 m)

Conservation status Generally common, but locally threatened in southern California

Length 8 in. (20 cm)

Wingspan 13 in. (33 cm)

Weight 1.4 oz. (40 g)

Diet Mainly insects and spiders, a few small lizards and tree frogs, and some nectar, fruits, and seeds

Nest Large ball of dry grasses and twigs, lined with feathers, built among the protective spines of a large cactus or thorn bush

Eggs 3–5, white to buff with brown speckling

Young Naked, blind, and helpless

that has regrown sometime after a fire. Males become more vocal in late February when the breeding season begins. They perch on the tops of cacti, bushes, or posts, delivering their loud, mechanical *chur chur chur* territorial song. This may also attract wandering females, but cactus wrens are monogamous and generally stay with the same mate for life.

Although some cactus wrens will nest in thorny shrubs and trees, such as mesquite or yucca, they usually favor cholla cacti or prickly pear, and occasionally tall saguaro cactus. Both sexes build the nest, which is typically placed in a fork between the spiny branches. The pair gathers a great mass of twigs and grass to weave a large, globular structure roughly the size of a soccer ball. The inside is hollow and lined with soft feathers. The female lays an average of four eggs. She incubates the eggs by herself for 16 days, and both sexes feed the helpless young when they hatch.

While the female is busy incubating, the male curiously starts building a second nest. When the first brood are able to fly—which takes about three weeks—the female helps complete the second nest and lays another clutch of eggs. The male may then start building a third nest. In all, he may build six nests, but it is quite rare for a pair of cactus wrens to successfully rear more than three broods in one season.

Adopted as an emblem of the desert state of Arizona in 1931, the cactus wren is common throughout most of its range. Coastal development in southern California is destroying large areas of the chaparral scrub that is favored by a local population of the species and is threatening its future. Elsewhere in the southwestern United States and Mexico, the cactus wren appears to be flourishing.

SEE ALSO

Passerines • Wrens and Dippers

California Condor

One of the biggest birds in North America, the California condor (*Gymnogyps californianus*) is also one of the rarest. In the early 1980s, it was on the verge of extinction, with just 22 birds left alive in the world. Today its numbers are increasing slowly, but it is still highly endangered.

The California condor is basically a giant vulture—a bird of prey specialized for eating dead animals. It is closely related to the similar but more widespread Andean condor (*Vultur gryphus*), and it has similarly enormous wings displaying outspread feathers at the tips. It has the widest wingspan of any North American bird, up to 9 feet (2.75 m). Its plumage is black, apart from the wings, which in adults have a white bar on the top and a large white patch on the underside. As with many vultures, its head and neck are virtually free of feathers, with pinkish skin that flushes to orange when the bird is excited. This is important for communication, for a condor has no specialized syrinx (vocal apparatus), so its vocalizations are limited to a variety of growls, grunts, and hisses.

Once widespread throughout North America, the California condor has suffered badly from habitat destruction and hunting. It had retreated to the Pacific coast by 1800, and by the 1970s, it was restricted to just a small area of California. In 1987, it was close to extinction, so the last free-ranging birds were caught and transferred to a captive breeding facility as a last-resort effort to save the species. Since 1992, however, a number of captive-bred condors have been successfully reared and released back into the wild in the deserts of California, Mexico, and Arizona, especially in Grand Canyon National Park.

They spend much of their time either perched on rocky crags or soaring in broad, slow circles on rising warm air currents. These currents may be from updrafts created by wind blowing against cliff faces and mountain ridges, or thermals of warm air currents that rise from heat reflected off the sun-warmed ground. The condor's long, broad wings are modified for this style of flight, with their splayed wingtip feathers that reduce turbulence and increase the efficiency of lift. They allow the bird to ride the air currents for hours with barely a wingbeat, so it uses very little energy. It soars in circles to remain within a thermal, steadily gaining altitude and searching for carrion, before gliding across country to find another thermal.

◀ The condor's naked head is an adaptation to its habit of delving deep within a carcass to feed, since head feathers like those of other birds would soon become matted with blood. The wing tags indicate that this bird is being monitored by conservationists.

Scientific name *Gymnogyps californianus*

Order Falconiformes

Family Cathartidae

Range Originally along the entire Pacific coast of North America and the southwestern desert states but now restricted to a few sites in California and Arizona

Habitat Arid and semi-arid deserts with cliffs and bare rock

Conservation status Critically endangered

Length 46–55 in. (117–140 cm)

Wingspan Up to 9 ft. (2.75 m)

Weight 20–24 lb. (9–11 kg)

Diet Carrion (dead animals)

Nest On protected bare rock cliff ledges, or occasionally in tall trees

Eggs 1–2, bluish-white

Young Downy, gray

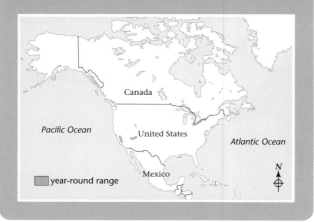

A condor may cover more than 150 miles (240 km) a day in this manner, scanning the ground for food. It targets large, fresh carcasses, such as those of deer, often locating them by observing the activity of smaller scavengers such as turkey vultures (*Cathartes aura*). Other scavengers may welcome the arrival of the much stronger condor, which is able to open up any carcass by ripping through even the thickest hide with its powerful hooked bill. As it feeds on the carcass, it often probes its head deep inside the body cavity.

California condors do not breed until they are about six years old, but they may live for more than fifty years. They pair for life, raising a family of one or sometimes two young just every other year. The female lays her eggs on a bare yet protected rock ledge, often within a crevice or small cave on a steep cliff, and both parents take turns incubating them for 54 to 58 days. When the young hatch, they are covered with grayish down and, although they grow black wing and body feathers before they fledge at the age of five to seven months, they keep their gray head plumage until they are ready to breed themselves.

Since the mid-1980s, when there were just eight California condors left in the wild, the outlook for this species has improved dramatically. Reintroduced birds started breeding for the first time in spring 2002, and there are now around three hundred individuals living in the southwestern United States and Mexico. Some birds have died from collisions with power lines, while others are killed by lead poisoning from eating game left by hunters using lead bullets. The overall population continues to increase, however, and one day it may reach a point at which the species can be taken off the federally endangered species list.

SEE ALSO

Birds of Prey • Turkey Vulture

Canada Goose

With its jet black head and neck and distinctive white chinstrap, the Canada goose (*Branta canadensis*) is the most easily identified of all the geese found in North America. It is also among the most common and familiar birds throughout most of Canada and the United States, as well as in several other parts of the world, where introduced Canada geese have flourished.

All Canada geese have the same unmistakable head and neck pattern, with a black bill and eyes, and a white undertail and rump. The sexes are alike, and juveniles resemble adults. Apart from this general similarity, however, there are several local plumage variations. In some populations, the white chinstrap is divided in two by a black stripe beneath the head. Some populations have a narrow white ring at the base of the black neck, while others do not. The back is

always brown with fine pale barring, but the underparts range from light gray or cream to chestnut brown, with the darker forms occurring farther west. Their body size also varies considerably, with the largest weighing three times as much as the smallest.

All these variations led taxonomists to recognize eleven local races, or subspecies, although populations are highly variable, and many individuals could not be easily identified to this level. The four smallest races, which breed on the Arctic tundra, are now considered as a separate species, known as the cackling goose (*Branta hutchinsii*). The most northerly breeding Canada geese nest in northern Canada and parts of Alaska. The

▼ Powerful fliers, Canada geese may migrate vast distances from their northern breeding grounds to spend the winter in milder regions to the south.

Scientific name *Branta canadensis*

Order Anseriformes

Family Anatidae

Range Arctic and temperate North America; introduced to Europe and New Zealand

Habitat Grassland near water, from Arctic tundra to city parks; also farmland, especially in winter

Conservation status Common

Length 30–43 in. (76–109 cm)

Wingspan 50–67 in. (127–170 cm)

Weight 6.6–20 lb. (3–9 kg)

Diet Grasses, sedges, seeds, berries, and aquatic plants

Nest Large, open cup of dry grass, moss, and lichen, lined with soft down, built near water

Eggs 2–8, cream

Young Well developed at hatching, covered with down and able to see; capable of swimming and gathering food within 24 hours

breeding range extends south to Nevada, Colorado, Tennessee, and North Carolina, and in winter, northern birds migrate as far south as the Gulf coast and northern Mexico. Wherever they occur, they rarely stray far from water.

Feeding Flocks

Canada geese are almost exclusively vegetarian and, unlike most waterfowl, they feed mainly on land, cropping grass with their finely saw-edged bills and eating a wide variety of leaves, flowers, stems, roots, seeds, and berries in summer. They also feed on the water, dabbling like many ducks to reach aquatic vegetation. Since many of the leafy materials have little food value, the birds may spend more than twelve hours a day feeding to get all the nutrients they need.

In winter, they often find spilled grain, beans, and rice on farmland. If such energy-rich foods are plentiful, the geese tend to feed in the fields for a few hours early in the day and then retreat to the safety of a secure roost by a lake or large river. They feed and roost in flocks of up to several thousand in their winter habitats, often in the company of other species. These mixed species flocks are not always harmonious, however, and the birds regularly confront each other with aggressive displays, bobbing their heads up and down on their long, flexible necks.

In spring, most Canada geese move slowly northward, advancing as the snow retreats north over several weeks until they reach their breeding grounds. The southward fall migration, triggered by the first freeze, is much quicker, and some radio-tracked birds have been known to complete the approximately 600-mile (1,000-km) journey from northern Quebec to the East Coast of the United States in a single day. They fly with powerful wingbeats in long, straggling V-formations, usually with a chorus of loud, resonant, honking calls. Formation flying saves energy, since each trailing bird flies in

REGULATION AND BEHAVIOR

PREDATOR AND PREY

Ground-nesting waterfowl make tempting prey for ground predators, and the Canada goose is no exception. In the far north, its main enemy is the Arctic fox, which may rely on the summer nesting season to provide most of its food for the entire year. A Canada goose is no soft target, however. They are powerful birds, able to use their wings to inflict serious injuries, although they can usually drive away a fox by rearing up, opening their wings, and hissing loudly. A male may draw a predator away from the nest with a "distraction display" of vulnerability before reverting to more direct threats. Despite this, many eggs and young are lost each season, and only half the goslings survive to the age when they can fly.

the slipstream of the one in front, and they regularly change places to take on the more arduous role of leader.

Nesting Territories

Canada geese pair up with a mate in their second winter. Rival males challenge each other with head-pumping displays, honks, and hisses, and may even engage in physical combat. Once individual pair bonds have formed, the male and female will stay together for life—which may be as long as 24 years in the wild. They tend to nest in colonies on sites with easy access to open water, such as swamps, marshes, wet grasslands, or tundra. Each pair maintains its own nesting territory within the colony, which the male defends against any encroaching neighbors or predators. The ideal nest site provides a clear view of any intruders. The nest is a simple pile of

▼ The large bodies and stomachs of adult Canada geese enable them to feed mainly on vegetation that must be eaten in bulk to provide enough nutrition.

vegetation, which the female gathers, arranges to form a cup, and lines with feathers and down from her own breast.

The female starts incubating her eggs after the last is laid, to ensure that they all hatch at once, 23 to 30 days later. The young geese, known as goslings, are well developed and able to leave the nest soon after hatching. The whole family then sets out for a suitable rearing area with sufficient water, often walking a significant distance while the goslings feed on grasses and other plants along the way. The family then feeds together for six to nine weeks, until the young fledge and are able to fly. By this time, temperatures are usually falling, so after feeding intensively for a few days, several families join together to fly south for the winter.

Decline and Revival

In the late 1800s, the largest race of the Canada goose, which bred in the northern United States and southern Canada, was almost wiped out by hunting and egg

▲ Although they are able to feed themselves soon after hatching, the downy goslings make tempting targets for predators, and they rely on their parents for protection.

collecting. Throughout the 20th century, however, geese from captive flocks were reintroduced to the southern parts of their former range, and by degrees the wild populations recovered. Indeed, they are now so numerous in many urban and suburban areas—where they are protected from hunting and have few natural predators—that they are becoming a nuisance to some people. Hunting restrictions in some other regions have been relaxed in an attempt to reduce numbers, but it is likely that the Canada goose will remain widespread.

SEE ALSO

Migration • Snow Goose • Trumpeter Swan • Waterfowl

Cardinals

The cardinal family (Cardinalidae) of North and South America belongs to the order Passeriformes, also known as perching birds. The Cardinalidae name comes from one of its commonest member species, the northern cardinal (*Cardinalis cardinalis*). This bird's bright red plumage reminded early European settlers of the red robes of Catholic cardinals.

Cardinals are closely related to the family Thraupidae, or tanagers, and recent DNA studies suggest that the tanager species found in North America are more closely related to the Cardinalidae than they are to the rest of the Thraupidae.

One distinguishing feature of the Cardinalidae is their powerful, conical

▶ Pyrrhuloxias and northern cardinals are closely related and look quite similar. The male pyrrhuloxia (right) can be distinguished from female and juvenile northern cardinals by its curved, yellow bill and overall gray plumage.

bill, used to crush seeds. Although their bills resemble those of the seed-eating cardueline finches (siskins, goldfinches, and redpolls), cardinals also feed on insects and fruits, depending on the season.

Distribution in North America

Ten species of cardinals breed in the United States, and an additional three species, the crimson-collared grosbeak (*Rhodothraupis celaeno*), the yellow grosbeak (*Pheucticus chrysopeplus*), and the blue bunting (*Cyanocompsa parellina*), occur in the United States as vagrants from Mexico and farther south.

In the north, the rose-breasted grosbeak (*Pheucticus ludovicianus*) breeds through central Canada and along the Canadian border from North Dakota to Maine. Its Midwest and eastern territory reaches south to Georgia. Both the northern cardinal and the indigo bunting (*Passerina cyanea*) are found throughout the eastern part of the country. The painted bunting (*Passerina ciris*) has a southeastern coastal range from North Carolina down to Florida and a separate south-central range from the Gulf Coast west to New Mexico. The dickcissel (*Spiza americana*) occupies the most central range in the western Great Plains.

The blue grosbeak (*Passerina caerulea*) occurs across the southern states, from the Pacific to Atlantic oceans, and from North Dakota south to the Mexican border. The varied bunting (*Passerina versicolor*) occupies southwestern Texas and southeastern Arizona, while the pyrrhuloxia (*Cardinalis sinuatus*) is

Order Passeriformes

Family Cardinalidae

Number of genera 12

Number of species 43

Range Central Canada south to central South America

Size range Length 4.5–8.8 in. (11.5–22 cm); wingspan 8–12 in. (20–30 cm); weight 0.8–1.6 oz. (23–45 g)

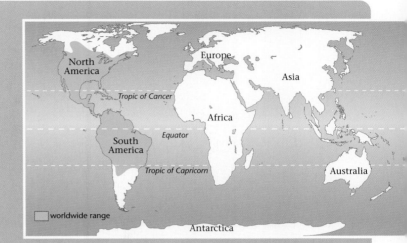

worldwide range

a resident of southern Texas, New Mexico, and Arizona. In the west, the black-headed grosbeak (*Pheucticus melanocephalus*) occurs in all the states of the western seaboard, extending east to the Dakotas, Nebraska, and Kansas, and south into Mexico. The lazuli bunting (*Passerina amoena*) covers much the same area but does not range as far east.

Leafy Habitats

Most suited to life among dense vegetation fairly low to the ground, cardinals court, breed, and feed in thickets and the brushy borders of fields, woodlands, and forests, as well as alongside roads and in suburban gardens and parks. Several species are associated with the foliage at the edges of streams, rivers, and swamps. Pyrrhuloxias and varied buntings often frequent mesquite thickets in arid desert areas.

Colorful Males

Cardinals range in size from the small buntings, which average 5.5 inches (14 cm) in length, to the two *Cardinalis* species, which have an average length of 8.8 inches (22 cm).

Males have colorful summer plumage. Apart from their conspicuous red coloring, their high, pointed crests make the northern cardinal and the pyrrhuloxia quite easy to

recognize. The male rose-breasted grosbeak has a bright pink bib, which contrasts with black upper parts and white underparts. The black-headed grosbeak has a breast and collar of bright cinnamon with a black head and back. The blue grosbeak, lazuli bunting, and indigo bunting are different shades of blue and can be distinguished from one another by variations in shade as well as wing and breast color. The male varied bunting has a blue head and rump and a bright red nape. Male painted buntings are the most colorful members of the family, with a red rump and underparts, a blue head, and a light-green back.

The male plumage of all species is more subdued during winter. Young males take up to two years to reach full adult plumage. The females are much dowdier, in various shades of brown, and are more difficult to identify.

Feeding and Diet

Cardinals generally feed on seeds, buds, and fruit in fall, winter, and spring and take advantage of the insect abundance in summer to boost their protein intake. They feed their chicks almost exclusively on insects. Most food is taken on the ground or by foraging among low thickets, although sometimes they fly up to catch insects on the

wing. Some species, such as the blue grosbeak and the rose-breasted grosbeak, have a summer diet that is half insects and half seeds. The black-headed grosbeak eats mainly spiders, insects, and snails in summer and is one of the few birds that is able to eat the poisonous monarch butterfly without suffering any ill effects.

The conical cardinal bill, which can crush tough mesquite beans, is also large enough to handle fruit in the fall, when the cardinals revert to a 90 percent vegetarian diet. Several cardinal species are attracted to garden bird feeders and can become dependent in winter on seeds such as millet and sunflower.

Courtship, Nesting, Eggs, and Young

In spring, North American Cardinalidae return from their winter territories, usually as individuals or in small groups, reaching their breeding areas between early April and mid-June. Each male establishes a territory by singing loudly from a prominent position to attract a mate and ward off other males. Although cardinals generally prefer to spend their time in the lower levels of dense foliage,

▲ Despite its gaudy plumage, the painted bunting is an extremely secretive bird, often heard singing from the depths of a shrub, without being visible. The capture of painted buntings for sale as caged birds has contributed to their steady decline.

males often sing their territorial songs from higher, exposed perches. Most cardinals are melodious singers.

Females often arrive from their migration a few days later than the males and choose the nesting site. In some cardinal species, both adults build the nest; in others, the female alone builds it. The nest is cup-shaped and is fairly loosely constructed of twigs, rootlets, leaves, and grasses, and lined with softer materials. It is usually placed low in a shrub or tree but is sometimes on the ground. The female lays between one and five eggs. In some species, the female alone incubates the eggs, while in others the male and female take turns.

After an average of between 10 and 14 days, the chicks hatch. They are naked and helpless, but between 8 and 14 days later, they will be able to leave the nest. Two weeks

▲ As in most cardinal species, the male blue grosbeak helps feed the hatchlings while they are in the nest. Blue grosbeaks sometimes also rear the young of brown-headed cowbirds (*Molothrus ater*), which often lay their eggs in the nests of blue grosbeaks.

after that, they will be able to fly. Several species go on to have second and even third broods. If this happens, the male may take over the feeding and welfare of the first brood, while the female sets about building a new nest and laying a new clutch of eggs.

LET'S INVESTIGATE

NORTHERN CARDINAL

As a year-round resident attracted to bird feeders, the northern cardinal is an ideal subject for a garden study project. Nearby shrubs and bushes, preferably conifers, provide good cover and reassurance. This bird's favorite feeder seeds are peanuts, sunflower seeds, safflower seeds, and millet. Hopper-style feeders with a wide tray are well suited to the northern cardinal, which likes plenty of room to feed. Projects could include month-by-month records of numbers, genders, and age groups of feeding birds, amounts and types of food items consumed, and social behavior. As well as keeping written records, it is possible to make a photographic or video record.

Migration

Cardinals are aggressively territorial during the breeding season, but after the young become independent, the adults are likely to join up with small flocks of the same species, and sometimes mixed species, to forage for food. Prior to migration, larger flocks of some species, such as the blue grosbeak, descend on grain fields and grasslands to feed.

Most cardinals fly south in late summer or early fall from their breeding areas in North America. Migration occurs at night, with birds using the stars to navigate. The black-headed grosbeak and the lazuli bunting migrate mainly to Mexico, although some lazuli buntings occasionally winter in southeastern Arizona. The varied bunting has a southern Texas population that may be resident year-round, but most birds of this species migrate to western Mexico. The

▼ Although considerably paler than her vivid red mate, the female northern cardinal is still readily identifiable by her olive-brown and rosy plumage, bright pink bill, and prominent crest. She often joins her mate in singing a duet.

painted bunting, the blue grosbeak, and the rose-breasted grosbeak all travel south to Mexico and Central America, while the indigo bunting flies south to Mexico, Central America, and the Caribbean Islands, or occasionally winters in southern Florida.

Some painted buntings make winter appearances in southern Florida, the Bahamas, and Cuba. The lazuli bunting migrates south in two stages, first congregating in large flocks in the Southwest to molt and then continuing on to Mexico. Northern cardinals and pyrrhuloxias do not migrate, although some pyrrhuloxias spread northward in New Mexico during winter.

A Mixed Future

None of the cardinals that breed in North America is currently considered endangered. The main threats come from loss of habitat. Human agricultural, urban, and industrial expansion have actually benefited several species in the past. The northern cardinal has been able to spread north because of forest clearance and the provisioning of bird-feeder seeds by people. Now, however, development in some places has reached a point at which it may threaten some cardinal species' numbers in the future. This is especially true for those breeding alongside rivers, streams, and coastlines, such as the indigo bunting, the painted bunting, and the lazuli bunting. The pyrrhuloxia may be similarly affected by loss of habitat from development in southwestern desert areas, and the rose-breasted grosbeak may eventually suffer from the fragmentation of forested areas.

SEE ALSO

Northern Cardinal • Passerines

BIRDS AND HUMANS

DICKCISSEL

Although DNA evidence confirms that it is a member of the Cardinalidae, the dickcissel differs from other cardinal species in several respects. It winters farther south than other North American–breeding cardinals, migrating through Mexico as far as Ecuador, Colombia, and French Guiana in South America. In the fall, dickcissels gather in vast flocks, moving south from the Great Plains. At their winter roosts, these flocks can number several millions. In Venezuela, sorghum and rice farmers have been known to wage chemical warfare on dickcissel flocks, spraying their roosts from the air with toxic agricultural chemicals. Although thousands of individuals have undoubtably been killed in this fashion, the dickcissel has maintained a stable population since 1980.

◄ Named for the sound of its call, the dickcissel is less striking than most of the cardinals. The male sports a distinctive black bib, white chin, and yellow breast, with a yellow line above the eye.

Chipping Sparrow

One of the smallest and most common species of sparrow, the chipping sparrow (*Spizella passerina*) is known for its trilling song, which has been likened to the sound of a sewing machine. It also produces a series of *chip-chip-chip* notes, for which it is named. It is easily recognizable in the breeding season by its bright chestnut crown, white face and throat, black eye line, tan back with black streaks, pale gray underparts, and black, conical beak. In winter, the crown is brown with black streaks.

In summer, the chipping sparrow is found throughout most of the United States, apart from the southern Great Plains and Florida. It winters in the southern states and down into Mexico, generally favoring areas where January temperatures remain above freezing.

This sparrow's most common natural habitat is along the edges and in clearings of dry, open woodlands with a grassy groundcover. In northern states and mountainous terrain, it occurs in open pine forests. It has readily adapted to urban areas, where it is attracted to bird feeders, and often nests close to houses, particularly in ornamental conifers.

During the breeding season, the chipping sparrow's diet consists mainly of insects. After nesting, family groups forage through

▼ The chipping sparrow used to be called the hairbird, because it often lines its nest with horse hair. Because of a decline in the horse population, it will use any available hair, even plucking hair from sleeping dogs.

Scientific name *Spizella passerina*

Order Passeriformes

Family Emberizidae

Range Eastern Alaska, southern Canada, and United States except southern Great Plains and Florida in summer; southernmost states, Mexico, and Central America in winter

Habitat Open woodlands, urban yards and parks, fringes of rivers, lakes, and forests

Conservation status Common

Length 5–6 in. (12–15 cm)

Wingspan 7–9 in. (18–23 cm)

Weight 0.39–0.53 oz. (11–15 g)

Diet Predominantly insects in breeding season, seeds in winter

Nest Loosely woven open cup of weeds and dead grass, lined with fine grasses and animal hair and placed in small tree or shrub

Eggs 2–7, pale blue with dark blotches

Young Helpless at hatching with tufts of down

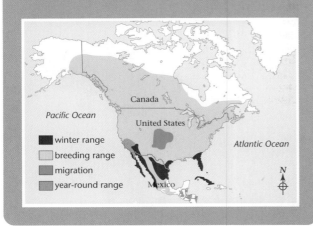

the fields and forest edges, sometimes associating with other family groups to locate food more efficiently. They move across the ground and through low bushes looking for prey, occasionally flying up to catch insects on the wing. Seeds form the major part of their diet in winter, and the species regularly visits gardens where seed and other food is provided.

After wintering in the south, the chipping sparrow reaches its northern breeding territories sometime between March and May. Males sing to court females and establish territories that they defend from intruders and competitors. The female builds a cup-shaped nest of dead grass and weed stalks, lined with fine grasses and animal hair, typically in a conifer. The male feeds the female, while she incubates between two and seven eggs for up to 14 days. Around the time that eggs are laid, the female develops a brood patch, a temporary bare spot on her abdomen, full of blood vessels. The brood patch helps transfer heat more efficiently to the eggs. Around 14 days after hatching, the fledglings are capable of sustained flight.

The chipping sparrow's population is probably several times greater than it was in pre-Columbian America, because of the creation of open areas by forest clearance. Numbers dropped dramatically around 1900, partly because of competition from introduced European house sparrows (*Passer domesticus*). Now, losses and gains probably cancel each other out. The chipping sparrow benefits from the reforestation of old fields and logged areas in the Southeast, where it now tends to outnumber field sparrow (*Spizella pusilla*) populations. With a life span of nine or ten years, and two or three broods a year, chipping sparrow populations seem to be stable for now.

SEE ALSO

Dark-eyed Junco • Passerines • Snow Bunting • Sparrows and Buntings

Colonies

A visit to a large breeding colony of birds can be a memorable experience. On the Bass Rock off the coast of Scotland, more than eighty thousand northern gannets (*Morus bassanus*) jostle for space in an area the size of a football stadium. Nesting just outside pecking range of each other, the goose-sized seabirds are so densely packed together that their white plumage makes the entire top of the rock appear white from a distance. The air is full of gannets coming and going with food for their young, and the cacophony of their harsh cries—and the scent of their droppings—can be almost overwhelming.

Spectacular colonies such as this are relatively rare, but colonial nesting behavior is common among birds. Roughly one in eight bird species breeds in this way, rather than in secluded pairs like many familiar backyard birds. They include a wide range of species, from tiny cave-nesting swiftlets to powerful vultures. Many colonial species are seabirds, like the northern gannet and a variety of auks, terns, gulls, shearwaters, and albatrosses. The colonial habit is also

▼ A pair of northern gannets perform a "sky-pointing" display to proclaim ownership of their nesting site within the huge, densely packed breeding colony.

common among many waterbirds such as herons, storks, pelicans, and flamingos. Some birds of prey breed in colonies, as do many swifts and swallows, and so do a variety of crows, starlings, sparrows, and weavers.

Such nesting colonies may blanket nearly the entire ground surface on an island or beach, occupy every ledge of a cliff, festoon a group of trees, or take over an abandoned building or roof space. The smallest colonies may consist of just a few pairs of birds, often well spaced out, while the largest may have thousands or even millions of pairs, packed together as tightly as possible. However, all colonies have one thing in common: the birds are in regular communication, to the point at which they may not be able to breed at all without the stimulus of social interaction.

Neighbors and Rivals

True colonies assemble for the purpose of breeding, although many species roost together in large, densely packed groups at night, especially in winter. Some of these sociable roosters also breed colonially, but many others disperse to nest on their own in well-spaced territories, coming back together again only when the breeding season is over.

The reasons why some species breed colonially are not always clear, especially given that there are several disadvantages to nesting in such close contact with neighbors

▲ The social weaver (*Philetairus socius*) of southern Africa breeds and roosts in a giant communal nest that may have a hundred or more cavities, one for each pair.

BIRDS AND HUMANS

VANISHED COLONIES

The largest bird colonies ever recorded were those of the passenger pigeon (*Ectopistes migratorius*), which once bred in huge numbers in the eastern United States. In the 18th century, the total population was estimated at five billion, making it the most common bird in the world. It nested in immense colonies of several million pairs, covering many square miles of woodland. Each tree contained up to one hundred nests. Throughout the 19th century, however, uncontrolled hunting caused a catastrophic population decline. As their colonies became smaller, the birds lacked the degree of social stimulus that they needed to breed successfully. When the last wild flock of 250,000 or more was destroyed in 1896—in a single day—the fate of the species was sealed, and within 20 years the passenger pigeon was extinct.

and rivals. Space is tight, and there is intense competition for every square inch. Rival pairs may trespass on each other's territory, steal nesting material, or even take over completely. Disputes and even fights are common. Nests may be hard to locate among the mass of birds, and nestlings may suffer from being jostled or even attacked by the neighbors.

A colony can more readily attract predators and nest robbers, which will lurk on the fringes, ready to take advantage of any lapse in security. Crows and skuas can frequently be seen near seabird colonies, watching for a chance to swoop down and steal an egg or a nestling. A colony can also facilitate parasites and disease transmission, especially if the same site is used every year. Bank swallows (*Riparia riparia*), for example, nest in colonies consisting of many burrows excavated in sandy cliffs. The colonies attract large numbers of bloodsucking fleas, which breed rapidly, lie dormant in the burrows all winter when the birds have migrated to warmer regions, and emerge when the birds return to breed in spring. The old burrows are often so heavily infested that the bank swallows are forced to dig new ones.

ADAPTATION AND DIVERSITY

CAVE COLONIES

The tiny cave swiftlets of Asia are miniature relatives of the swifts that hunt small flying insects in the northern skies in summer. They nest in big, tightly packed colonies in caves, attaching their bracketlike nests to the rock near the cave roof. Their nests are made from plant material and held together with the birds' sticky saliva, which hardens like glue. The nests of some species consist almost entirely of this hardened saliva, and they are traditionally collected as the main ingredient of Chinese bird's nest soup.

It is so dark in the nesting caves that the swiftlets cannot see their way, but they have evolved the ability to navigate by echolocation, like bats. As each bird flies through the cave, it emits a rapid stream of clicks and instinctively uses the echoes reflected off the cave walls to form a spatial mental image of its surroundings. In this way, a swiftlet not only finds its way through the cave in total darkness but also locates its own nest among thousands of others.

▶ Built in permanent darkness, but revealed here by flashlight, the nests of the Seychelles swiftlet (*Aerodramus elaphrus*) are simple half-cups cemented to the rock.

▶ For centuries, colonial guanay cormorants have been returning to breed on Independencia Island, Peru, building up an immense depth of dried, phosphate-rich guano.

Limited Options

One motive for colonial breeding can be a shortage of suitable nesting sites, forcing the birds to crowd together in the few places available to them. Over many generations, they may become so used to this that they may exclusively nest in tight colonies, even if their numbers are reduced to the point at which they could spread out.

This is common among seabirds, which need to nest as close to the water as possible because it is the source of their food. A coastal cliff or island is ideal, and since the birds do not have to defend food resources on land—one reason that so many other species claim a large territory—each pair can make do with a small patch of bare rock in the midst of a dense colony.

Many seabirds are so highly specialized for life at sea that they are virtually helpless on land. They cannot risk nesting on sites that are readily accessible to ground predators such as foxes. This is particularly true of shearwaters (ocean birds related to albatrosses). They shuffle over the ground on their bellies and often cannot get into the air unless there is a stiff breeze or they are able to dive off a cliff ledge. Many shearwater species nest beneath rocks, or in burrows that they dig themselves, on islands that are cut off from the dangers of the mainland. Suitable sites can be scarce, and as a result, they are occupied by huge numbers of birds. Around 30,000 pairs of Cory's shearwaters (*Calonectris diomedea*) nest on the Atlantic island of Selvagem Grande off North Africa, and in the past the colony consisted of well over 100,000 pairs.

These seabird colonies may be reoccupied every breeding season for hundreds or even thousands of years, so the entire landscape is shaped by them. The Chilean islands occupied by guanay cormorant (*Phalacrocorax bougainvillii*) colonies are famous for the deep deposits of guano (fossilized bird droppings) that have built up over centuries in the very dry climate. The deposits are so thick that they were mined for use as fertilizer in the 19th century.

Mutual Defense

Although some seabird breeding colonies are inaccessible to land predators, other species are more exposed to attack. For this reason, mutual defense may also be a motive for nesting in close company. Many terns (slender, gull-like seabirds) nest in colonies on beaches and clifftops that are sometimes vulnerable to egg thieves and predators. They defend their nests by swooping down and pecking at trespassers, including people. A concerted attack by several terns is often enough to drive away a potential predator. Many other birds will join forces to harass aerial predators such as crows and birds of prey, and colonial nesting ensures that there are plenty of recruits for these airborne operations.

Simply nesting close together can also improve security. An isolated nest is exposed on all sides, but four nests in a square are each exposed to attack from only one side. The bigger the colony, the less the risk, especially for birds nesting in the center. In most colonial species, the older birds have a higher social status and defend territories in the heart of the colony, while lower-status pairs nest on the vulnerable fringes. The sheer number of nests also means that the probability of being attacked is greatly reduced, and few predators hunt in sufficient numbers to decimate a whole colony.

Many species that have few serious enemies still nest in colonies. For example, the griffon vultures of Asia and Africa are big enough to defend themselves, yet they breed in cliff

POPULATIONS AND ECOSYSTEMS

FLAMINGO LAKES

The eastern branch of Africa's highly volcanic Great Rift Valley is dotted with shallow lakes that are rich in dissolved sodium carbonate, or soda. Some lakes contain so much soda that very few species of living things can survive in them, but those species that can withstand the conditions tend to swarm in vast numbers. They provide food for huge flocks of flamingos, which strain the lake water through meshlike filters in their bills to catch the tiny algae and various aquatic animals. The flamingos also breed on these lakes. On Lake Natron in Tanzania, lesser flamingos (*Phoenicopterus minor*) form colonies of up to a million pairs (below). They crowd together in the shallows to incubate their eggs and raise their young in craterlike mud nests, relying on the surrounding poisonous water to discourage enemies such as jackals.

colonies of one hundred pairs or more. This suggests that there is yet another possible motive for nesting in such close company.

Information Exchange

This motive may be communication. Many birds that breed in colonies also forage together, either in flocks or by watching each other's movements. This social feeding habit is common among species that have unpredictable but locally abundant food supplies. Griffon vultures, for example, scavenge from the carcasses of large, recently killed animals such as antelopes. Finding such carcasses may not be easy, but once they are located, there is usually enough food for many birds. They watch each other intently as they soar over the plains, and when one bird locates food and starts to circle downward, neighboring birds follow its lead. Before long, there may be hundreds waiting their turn to pick at the bones.

Such birds benefit from foraging alongside each other, particularly the less-experienced individuals, which are able to shadow their elders and take advantage of their superior experience and skill. Breeding in a colony provides ample opportunities for this kind of learning. The breeding season is also the time when birds are most in need of reliable food supplies to provide for their young.

▲ In Africa, northern carmine bee-eaters (*Merops nubicus*) have been known to form breeding colonies of up to ten thousand pairs, each with its own nesting burrow excavated in soft earth.

LET'S INVESTIGATE

COLONY WATCHING

Several widespread birds breed in colonies within the United States. They include a variety of grebes, herons, terns, swifts, swallows, and martins. If such a breeding colony can be located in an area nearby, identify the birds and observe them as they interact at the colony. Do they cooperate to drive away enemies? Where do they go to feed? When they get there, do they feed together? Check a book or the Internet to find out what they eat and decide whether they might have to compete with each other for food. Try to figure out how breeding in a colony benefits each pair of birds and whether there any obvious drawbacks.

Many smaller birds that breed in colonies have the same group-foraging habit and probably follow each other to good food sources. Many species of swifts and swallows, for example, hunt airborne insects in groups that may be led by more experienced individuals. This habit has been observed in cliff swallows (*Petrochelidon pyrrhonota*), which nest colonially on cliffs and bridges throughout most of North America.

Some species may also communicate while they are at the colony, in ways that are not yet understood, passing on information in some way. Many breeding colonies are certainly very noisy at certain times of day. This communication may explain why birds such as herons and egrets breed in colonies, even though they hunt alone.

Mixed Motives

Older, more experienced birds have less to gain from information exchange, and it is possible that in some species, they may be adversely affected by competition with younger birds when feeding. However, since the more experienced pairs generally secure the best nest sites in the middle of the colony, they benefit from mutual defense.

▼ An isolated island off the coast of Peru provides a secure site for an otherwise vulnerable colony of ground-nesting Peruvian pelicans (*Pelecanus thagus*).

By contrast, young birds that nest on the fringes of a colony may not enjoy much extra security, but they have a lot to gain from such close proximity because they are less experienced at finding food. Consequently, the motives of the colony members could vary according to their age and where they nest in the colony. Each individual has its own reasons for being part of the colony, and these may change over time.

These motives may extend beyond the breeding season. Many colonial birds also roost in colonies at night when their young have left the nest, probably for the same reasons that they breed in colonies in summer. Even species that breed apart do this. Many shorebirds in particular occupy their own separate territories during the nesting season—frequently on Arctic tundra—but gather in massive roosts, often composed of several species, near the high tide line on their coastal wintering grounds. In such places, there is so much food available that the birds do not have to compete for it, and it is possible that if food were as easy to find on the tundra, they would breed in colonies there, as well.

For further discussion of bird families that live in large colonies, see:
> Albatrosses, Petrels, and Shearwaters • Auks • Flamingos • Gulls, Terns, and Skuas • Penguins • Swallows and Martins • Swifts

For related discussions on colonial living in birds, see:
> Defense • Nests • Territories

Common Grackle

One of the United States' most numerous birds, the common grackle (*Quiscalus quiscula*) gets its name from the Latin word *graculus*, which means "jackdaw." Its plumage, legs, and daggerlike bill are black, and its feathers are iridescent. In different regions, they may look bronze, purple, or blue-green in the sunlight. The eyes are pale yellow. Juveniles have brown plumage and eyes. The common grackle often nests in noisy colonies, and its migratory flocks can number more than a million birds.

The species is found in nearly all states east of the Rocky Mountains and is a permanent resident throughout much of its range. Those found in northern states and over the Canadian border during the breeding season migrate to southeastern states for the winter. The more southerly populations stay put or move closer to urban areas.

The common grackle prefers to forage in open areas, where it can find food on the ground. In the countryside, it inhabits open woodlands, marshes, and the fringes of rivers and lakes with some trees and shrubs where it can roost and nest. Its numbers have increased considerably as the

▶ The juvenile common grackle has dull brown plumage for the first few months of its life but undergoes a complete post-juvenile molt, usually in August, and emerges with full iridescent plumage.

Scientific name *Quiscalus quiscula*

Order Passeriformes

Family Icteridae

Range Most of Canada and the United States, east of the Rocky Mountains

Habitat Open areas with some trees, open woodland, swamps, agricultural areas, and urban parks

Conservation status Common

Length 11–13.4 in. (28–34 cm)

Wingspan 17–18.5 in. (43–47 cm)

Weight 3.25–4.6 oz. (92–130 g)

Diet Insects and other invertebrates, small fish, amphibians, mice, and other birds; in winter, mainly grains and seeds, some fruit

Nest Cup-shaped, made from woody stems, leaves, and grasses, lined with mud, fine grass, and animal hair

Eggs 4–7, light blue to pale brown, often with dark markings

Young Juveniles have brown plumage and eyes

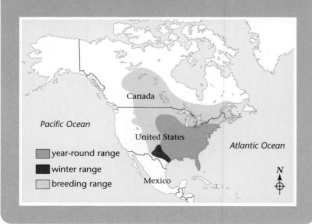

human population has cleared forests for farming and created urban areas with open spaces and ornamental trees.

The common grackle is omnivorous, foraging over the ground for insects, spiders, worms, and other invertebrates, as well as seeds such as acorns and fallen grain on farmland. Along lakes and rivers, it wades in the shallows to catch small fish and frogs and even catches bats in flight on occasions. Other prey include fledglings and much smaller birds of other species. Huge autumn migratory grackle flocks pose a real threat to cereal crops, particularly corn, and some farmers shoot or poison them.

After leaving their winter retreats near the end of February, pairs bond at the breeding sites in early spring with mutual displays and singing. The female builds a nest on her chosen site, usually between 2 and 12 feet (0.6–3.7 m) above the ground, often in a conifer. She incubates the eggs for between 12 and 14 days. Around half the chicks survive to adulthood.

The common grackle is a common and widespread bird that readily adapts to new conditions by surviving on a highly variable diet. It is killed in large numbers by farmers and local authorities in areas where it badly damages crops, and it is prey to several different predators, including snakes, birds of prey, cats, foxes, and raccoons. Numbers have fallen since 1970 in the eastern parts of its range but have increased significantly in its western range, partly due to the planting of ornamental trees in urban areas. With a life span of between 8 and 12 years, it remains one of the United States' most common and least threatened birds.

SEE ALSO

American Blackbirds and Orioles
• Baltimore Oriole • Brown-headed Cowbird • Eastern Meadowlark
• Passerines • Red-winged Blackbird

Common Moorhen

The common moorhen (*Gallinula chloropus*) is a familiar sight on many lowland ponds, lakes, and wetlands, especially in summer. Appearing mainly black from a distance, adults have a yellow-tipped, bright red bill, a distinctive red frontal shield that extends over the forehead, and sturdy, mostly greenish-yellow legs with very long toes. At closer range, it is dark brown above and slate gray below, with narrow white bars on its flanks, a white patch beneath its tail, and red eyes. Immature birds are brown with greenish-brown bills.

Widespread throughout temperate and tropical regions of the world, this species is resident in the warmer southern parts of the United States, from California to the Gulf coast and coastal Virginia. In the spring and summer, it also breeds throughout the lowlands well to the east of the prairies and north to the Great Lakes. These northern breeders migrate south in the fall to winter in the same regions as the southern residents, or move farther south into Central America.

Common moorhens are often seen swimming on the water with a head-bobbing, tail-flicking action, or walking on top of and among aquatic plants with seemingly nervous and jerky movements. They frequently venture well away from wet areas to feed, but at any hint of danger, they run back to open water or duck into cover with lowered heads, their wings flapping, giving an abrupt *kekuk* alarm call. If a moorhen is threatened or disturbed on the water, it will sometimes dive and stay nearly submerged among aquatic plants, with just its head visible above the surface.

Common moorhens eat a wide variety of food, including pondweeds, berries, seeds, insects, spiders, snails, and worms. They sometimes pick at the bodies of dead animals, and they may even consume the eggs of other birds during the nesting season. They often feed while swimming, usually by dipping their heads beneath the water or by sifting food floating on the surface. Their extremely long toes spread their weight over a broad

▼ The bright red and yellow bill of the moorhen is very distinctive. This bird is incubating eggs on a nest built of dead reeds at the edge of a pond.

Scientific name *Gallinula chloropus*

Order Passeriformes

Family Rallidae

Range Widespread through eastern United States in breeding season; year-round in parts of South and Southwest; also in Caribbean, Mexico, Central and South America, Europe, Africa, and Asia

Habitat Ponds, lakes, quiet streams and rivers, freshwater marshes, and nearby grasslands

Conservation status Common

Length 13–14 in. (33–36 cm)

Wingspan 21–24 in. (53–61 cm)

Weight 9–16 oz. (255–454 g)

Diet Aquatic plants, seeds, fruit, insects, tadpoles, carrion

Nest Deep cup of twigs and stems lined with fine grasses, floating in shallows, among waterside vegetation, or in a bush or tree

Eggs 5–11, buff with brown and gray blotches

Young Covered with gray-black down except for naked red crown and wings; can swim soon after hatching

area, enabling them to forage by walking on top of floating vegetation. On land, they search for food among damp soil and grass and by climbing through dense vegetation.

In summer, they usually forage alone or in family groups, but outside the breeding season, common moorhens often form small, loose feeding flocks, especially when they have migrated away from their breeding areas. In warmer regions where the birds do not migrate, pairs may stay on their breeding territories throughout the year and are less gregarious.

Migratory individuals form new pair-bonds each year when they return to their breeding sites. Rival males display aggressively with lowered heads, raised tails, and arched wings, giving loud, explosive *kurr-uck* territorial calls. They frequently fight and chase each other in an attempt to show their dominance. Pairs engage in bowing and mutual preening displays. Both sexes build the nest, usually on the mud among waterside vegetation and at the edge of a pool or quiet backwater, sometimes on a floating mat of sticks anchored by reed stems, or occasionally in a nearby bush or even a tree up to 25 feet (8 m) above the ground.

The female lays a clutch of five to nine eggs, and both adults take turns to incubate them for three weeks. The downy young are very well developed when they hatch, able to follow the female as she forages and supplies them directly with food. Young birds can forage for themselves when they are around 25 days old, but the adults keep feeding them until they are able to fly at 40 to 50 days. Individuals may live for up to 10 years in the wild, and despite some loss of habitat through wetland drainage, they are not threatened in any way.

SEE ALSO

American Coot • Cranes, Rails, and Bustards

Glossary

brood: all the young hatched and raised during one breeding attempt by a single female bird

brood parasitism: breeding behavior in which a female bird deceives birds of another species into raising its young, at the expense of the host bird's own offspring

clutch: all the eggs laid at one breeding attempt by a single female bird

colony: a group of breeding birds of a single species that nest close to one another

DNA: deoxyribonucleic acid; the molecules in all cell nuclei that contain genetic information

dominance hierarchy: a social order in which each bird recognizes its place in relation to dominant and subordinate birds

dormancy: a state of biological inactivity

down: the soft, fluffy feathers found on newly hatched chicks and underneath the main feathers of adult birds

echolocation: the act of emitting high frequency sound waves to locate surrounding objects

ecological niche: the range of habitat conditions and resources in which a particular species is able to live

evolution: the process by which species change in form and genetic composition over a long period of time, as a result of natural selection

extinction: the dying out of a species

fledge: to be completely feathered and fly for the first time

fledgling: a young bird that has just left the nest

forage: to wander in search of food

incubation: the warming of eggs to aid the development and hatching of young

insectivore: an organism that feeds on insects

invertebrate: an animal that lacks a spinal column (backbone)

juvenile: a young bird that has grown its first fully functional feathers

lek: a place where male birds gather to attract females through competitive display

migration: regular travel from one area to another as seasons or conditions change

molt: to shed old feathers and replace them with new ones

monogamous: mating with a single partner

nestling: a young bird that lives in the nest from hatching to fledging

nocturnal: active during the night

parasitism: living off another living organism, often in a way that harms the host

pesticide: a chemical that kills pests and other animals upon ingestion

plumage: a bird's feathers

polygamous: mating with more than one partner in a single breeding season

race: a subspecies, or population of a species residing in a particular geographic area, having characteristics distinct from other populations of the same species

raptor: a bird of prey that hunts in daytime

retina: the multilayered membrane that lines the eye; it receives images from the lens and converts them to chemicals and nerve signals that travel through the optic nerve to the brain

roost: a site where birds sleep

scavenge: to feed on dead and decaying plant or animal matter

syrinx: a bird's vocal organ, located where the trachea joins the bronchi

talon: the claw of a bird of prey

taxonomy: the science of classifying living organisms into groups based on relationships and similar features

tendon: a band of fibrous tissue that joins a muscle to a bone

territory: an area defended by a bird against others of the same species

thermal: a rising column of warm air on which birds gain height and soar without using much energy

vagrant: a bird that has wandered outside its normal range

vertebrate: an animal with a spinal column (backbone)

Index

Numbers in *italic* refer to illustrations.
Numbers in **boldface** refer to a
complete article.

Index

Guide to Common Species Names

This list, which includes alternate forms of common bird names, is designed to help users find articles on birds that interest them. This is not a complete list of birds discussed in Birds of the World. *For the complete list of species mentioned in this reference work, see the indexes in volume 11.*